Every
with J

Love Came to Bring us Home

'Where sin increased,
grace increased all the more'
Romans 5:20

Selwyn Hughes
Revised and updated by Mick Brooks
FURTHER STUDY: IAN SEWTER

© CWR 2013. Dated text previously published as *Every Day
with Jesus: East of Eden* (November/December 2003) by CWR.
This edition revised and updated for 2013 by Mick Brooks.

CWR, Waverley Abbey House, Waverley Lane, Farnham, Surrey GU9 8EP, UK
Tel: 01252 784700 Email: mail@cwr.org.uk
Registered Charity No. 294387. Registered Limited Company No. 1990308.

Unless otherwise stated, all Scripture quotations are from the Holy Bible,
New International Version. © International Bible Society.

Cover image: Getty/Photographer's Choice/David Muir
Quiet Time image: sxc.hu/memoossa

Printed in England by Linney Print

MIX
Paper from
responsible sources
FSC® C015900
www.fsc.org

CWR

A word of introduction ...

Whilst reviewing this issue I have been forcibly struck by several truths. At times, life can feel like a complicated maze and when we tune into the underlying restlessness of our souls we discover a thirst and ache that nothing in this world can satisfy. But no matter how overwhelming life's realities might seem, when I become aware of them, I always end up back at the Cross. This is not because of my own resourcefulness, but because God had a plan from the beginning. The first couple were expelled from the Garden of Eden, but not forgotten.

In this issue Selwyn tackles many common struggles, reminding us that although we often live 'east of Eden' as a result of our own choices, God has a plan to guide us through the maze of life and bring us back home.

The phrase East of Eden was first popularised in 1952 by John Steinbeck in his novel of the same title. James Dean starred in a later silver screen adaptation. It is said that Steinbeck drew inspiration from the first few chapters of Genesis. We know for sure that he drew his title from Genesis 4:16 'and Cain went out from the presence of the Lord, and dwelt in the Land of Nod, on the east of Eden' (KJV).

In this final issue of 2013 we will explore the varied difficulties of living East of Eden, being encouraged afresh by God's unconditional love for us that brings us out of the maze, and safely home.

Sincerely yours in His name,

Mick

Mick Brooks, Consulting Editor

Expelled - but not abandoned

FOR READING & MEDITATION - GENESIS 3:20-24

'After he drove the man out, he placed on the east side of the Garden of Eden cherubim ... to guard the way to the tree of life.' (v24)

A s we look at this world – a world that often seems filled with distress and disappointment – we cannot help but feel that life is strangely poisoned at the fount. Everything that lives is subject to death and disease – animals, birds, fish, flowers and, of course, human life also.

When Mrs C.F. Alexander wrote the hymn *All things bright and beautiful* she was looking only at certain things – the things which were 'bright and beautiful'. It wasn't all of creation that she had in view. She was being selective. There are many things in creation that are *not* at all beautiful – floods, earthquakes, volcanic eruptions, tsunamis, and so on. The apostle Paul, who saw the world in its true perspective, said, 'We know that the whole creation has been groaning as in the pains of childbirth' (Rom. 8:22). Who can doubt it? When Paul looked at creation he looked at all of it, and his faith remained strong and secure.

Why is the physical and human creation in such dire straits? The answer is found in the passage we have read today. When God created Adam and Eve He placed them in a garden of astonishing beauty. But they failed to live in accordance with His commands and were expelled from that garden, never to return. God put cherubim, or 'celestial bouncers', at the exit to ensure they would not be able to return. Their future lay east of Eden. Following their sin a curse was pronounced on the whole creation.

The good news, however, is this: though God banished Adam and Eve from the garden He did not abandon them. God, in government, excluded them from the garden; God, in grace, covered their nakedness with garments of skin. God judges sin but doesn't abandon the sinner.

FURTHER STUDY

John 9:1-38

1. Why was the blind man expelled?

2. How was he not abandoned?

O Father, how reassuring it is to be reminded that though You hate sin You do not lose Your love for the sinner. You are not against us for our sin, but for us against our sin. Thank You dear Father. Amen.

FOR READING & MEDITATION – GENESIS 3:14-19

'By the sweat of your brow you will eat your food until you return to the ground ...' (v19)

Following on from yesterday – that life seems strangely poisoned at the fount – we see today that three main consequences resulted from Adam and Eve's sin in the Garden of Eden: for the serpent, for Eve, and for Adam. The serpent, who may well have been a creature of great beauty prior to the Fall, was reduced to crawling through the dust. Eve was told that she would experience pain in child-bearing. From this we may assume, I think, that had she not sinned then child-bearing would have been painless. Adam was informed that because of his sin the ground would be cursed and he would find it resisting him as he sought to cultivate it in an effort to obtain food.

FURTHER STUDY

Isa. 14:11-15;
Isa. 15:1-9

1. How do we display an attitude of independence?

2. What is the result of trying to be independent of God?

These consequences for Adam and Eve were neither vindictive nor punitive but they did discourage them from thinking that their lives could ever work effectively unless they returned to the original design of being dependent on God. God introduced complications into the very core of their lives that were calculated to turn them back to Him in dependent trust. Adam and Eve's sin amounted to what we might call a 'declaration of independence', and now, by way of the curse, they were being put in the position where they would discover that life was meant to work one way and one way only – by dependence on God the Father.

The only explanation of why creation can be so bright and beautiful, yet so dark and ugly, is that it is suffering from the effects of an act of justice which God pronounced on the world after Adam and Eve's sin. Our world is a fallen world that sits under the justice of a good and righteous God, but a God in whose heart lie also the qualities of mercy and forgiveness.

My Father and my God, I am more grateful than words can convey that You are not only my justice but my Saviour also. All glory and honour be to Your name for ever. Amen.

Mixed emotions

FOR READING & MEDITATION - ROMANS 8:22-25

'... we ourselves, who have the firstfruits of the Spirit, groan inwardly as we wait eagerly for our adoption ...' (v23)

We continue reflecting on the fact that due to Adam and Eve's declaration of independence, the whole creation, to use the words of the apostle Paul, 'has been groaning as in the pains of childbirth' (v22). He goes on to say that not only is there a groan in creation but there is a groan also in the hearts of those who have 'the firstfruits of the Spirit'.

Over the years I have met many Christians who have ignored this truth, claiming that the heritage of a Christian is not a groan but joy. After all, such Christians say, is it not the second fruit of the Spirit? But to possess joy and yet at the same time be aware of an inward groan is the tension in which we as Christians live out our daily lives. If we experienced *only* joy in our hearts how strange that would be. How can a Christian go through the day indifferent to such horrors as the hunger of millions, the ravages of AIDS, the carnage of war, the threat of terrorism, and so on? Everyone whose eyes have been opened by Jesus through faith must surely groan within themselves as they tune in to the plight and the pain of suffering humanity. One thing is sure: those who deny that groan do not share the compassion of Jesus.

Not so long ago politicians talked about Utopia – an imaginary state with a perfect social and political system. But we have come to see that Utopia is a pipe-dream. There is no way back to the sinless state of the Garden of Eden. The only 'Utopia' is the one that lies up ahead which Jesus has gone to prepare for us and which the Bible calls heaven. Meanwhile we live with mixed emotions: joy because of our eternal salvation and a groan because the world is adrift from God.

FURTHER STUDY

Luke 10:21;
John 11:32-44;
2 Cor. 1:3-11

1. What emotions did Jesus experience?

2. How did Paul experience mixed emotions?

O Father, save me I pray from being unwilling to own these mixed emotions. I see that to deny the groan within me is to shut myself off from Your compassion. Please help me my Father. In Jesus' name. Amen.

Atheism: the most awful thing

FOR READING & MEDITATION - ROMANS 8:26-27
'We do not know what we ought to pray for, but the Spirit himself
intercedes for us with groans ...' (v26)

Not only is there a groan in creation and in the hearts of the people of God, but the verses before us today tell us God's Holy Spirit groans also. This is probably the most amazing thing of all – a groan in the heart of God. This is a most astonishing fact. Can you see what it means? God's heart aches for us all the time, longing to help us, filled with a desire to give us the strength and grace to overcome life in a fallen world.

Dr W.E. Sangster once asked a number of people what was the most awful thing they could think of. Some said it was their own death. A few said it was the permanent loss of their reason. Others said it was a third world war. Sangster agreed that these were awful possibilities but he claimed there was something even worse than them – atheism! Sheer atheism! The belief that behind this universe there is not the loving Father whom Jesus revealed but some blind impersonal force. That, said Sangster, is the most awful thing anybody could ever think of: 'that we do not matter, that we wink out, at the last, like a candle, that all our life ends in a handful of grey ashes'. Such a thought is awful because it is not true. Behind the universe, fallen and cursed because of sin, is a God who cares so much for us that He groans in His love for us and yearns to redeem us. 'The Spirit himself intercedes for us with groans that words cannot express.'

Christians know differently, however. We know that though God has to judge sin, the cross of His Son is a symbol of His groan for a wayward world. Be assured of this: at the centre of this fallen world a loving God is at work.

FURTHER STUDY

Gen. 6:1-8;
2 Pet. 3:1-9

1. What filled God's heart?

2. What is God's attitude to scoffers and atheists?

Read thro'

O Father, what a comfort it is to know that through Your Holy Spirit You are working to redeem and overcome the damage caused by the Fall. Unending love and mercy burns at the heart of all things. And I am its recipient. Thank You. Amen.

CWR Ministry Events
PLEASE PRAY FOR THE TEAM

ATE	EVENT	PLACE	PRESENTER(S)
ov	Nurturing Kingdom Values in Schools	Waverley Abbey House	Derek Holbird
Nov	Counselling Enquirers' Event	WAH	Counselling team
Nov	Life and Times of Jesus	WAH	Andy Peck
10 Nov	Bible Discovery Weekend	WAH	Philip Greenslade
-22 Nov	Introduction to Biblical Care and Counselling	WAH	Angie Coombes and team
Nov	Bible in a Day	Pilgrim Hall	Andy Peck
Nov	MBTI® (Basic) for Counselling Students	WAH	Lynn & Andrew Penson
-27 Nov	Coaching and Mentoring	WAH	Beverley Shepherd and Andy Peck
Nov Dec	Women's Advent Weekend - Dwelling with Him	WAH	Paula Buchel
Nov	Helping Survivors of Emotional/ Sexual Abuse	WAH	Heather Churchill
Dec	Helping Those Affected by Cancer	WAH	Sara Lister and Chris Lee
Dec	Women's Christmas Event - Christmas Expectations	PH	Paula Buchel
-27 Dec	Christmas House Party	PH	

lease also pray for students and tutors on our ongoing **BA in Counselling** rogramme at Waverley and Pilgrim Hall and our **Certificate and Diploma of hristian Counselling** and **MA in Integrative Psychotherapy** held at London chool of Theology.

or further details and a full list of CWR's courses, phone +44 (0)1252 784719 r visit the CWR website at www.cwr.org.uk Pilgrim Hall: www.pilgrimhall.com

God's last word

FOR READING & MEDITATION - JUDE 17-25

'To him who is able to keep you from falling and to present you before his glorious presence ... with great joy ...' (v24)

One of the reasons why people don't believe in a God of love is that they cannot connect the distress and problems of life with a God who is supposed to be all-loving. How many times have you heard someone remark, 'If there is a God of love then why are there so many problems in the world and why is there so much suffering?' Those who talk like that clearly, in my view, do not understand what the Bible reveals to us about creation. Let me try to make it clear: Adam and Eve's sin had a catastrophic effect on the whole of creation and has left us with a legacy that it is not easy to live with. I have heard some ask, 'Why would God respond in such a heavy and far-reaching way to a little thing like eating forbidden fruit?' That 'little' sin, as some may call it, was, in reality, the most tragic thing that could happen in a God-created universe – a created will resisting and rebelling against the will of the Creator. Inevitably there were consequences, and God's judgment and justice mean that now, instead of living in a world where there is nothing wrong with anything, we live in a world where there is something wrong with everything.

FURTHER STUDY

John 15:11;
John 16:20-24;
Rev. 21:1-7

1. What does Jesus give us?
2. What is God's last word?

Life east of Eden is difficult. We must face that reality and not shrink from it. Faith that is not based on realism will leave us immature. Hear the groan in creation. Hear the groan within yourself. Hear with wonder the Spirit making intercession for us with groaning which cannot be expressed in words. And always remember, as our text for today shows, that God's last word in His universe is not a groan but great joy!

Father, help me face the facts that lie behind the universe however unpleasant they may be. Life may be difficult in this fallen world but never too difficult when my hand is in Yours. Thank You Father. Amen.

'The man said, "The woman you put here with me - she gave me some fruit from the tree, and I ate it."' (v12)

The great writer Oswald Chambers once said, 'Life is more tragic than orderly.' What an insightful statement. His was not a faith nourished on ignorance and deliberately blind to the ugly realities of this suffering world. He faced the facts as they are and avoided the kind of hothouse religion some Christians prefer which only maintains its tenuous existence by ignoring challenging matters.

What awful burdens people have to bear in this fallen world. A happy, healthy young girl who was about to be married commented in a newspaper article, 'If only people would look at the world in the right way, they would see everything in it is beautiful.' Yet that same newspaper told of two murders, the rape of an elderly woman, the death of a little child from leukaemia, and several other tragedies.

FURTHER STUDY

Gen. 37:3-28

1. Describe the brothers' relationship.

2. What caused their problems?

It is time now to consider some of the hard things our mortal heart and flesh are called to bear east of Eden. Take first the problem of *disconnected relationships*. Today's reading shows that no sooner were Adam and Eve disconnected from God than they became estranged from each other. Notice how Adam diverted the blame as he said to God, 'The woman you put here with me – she gave me some fruit from the tree, and I ate it.' How do you think Eve must have felt as she heard Adam blame her for their predicament? I would imagine, estranged and disconnected from him. Eve in turn blamed the serpent for their plight. Sin caused separation in the first human relationship, and this issue of estrangement is one that almost everyone has to deal with at some point or another. I have no hesitation in saying that some of the most acute pains we bear east of Eden come from conflict in relationships.

Heavenly Father, I am aware that estrangement constitutes one of the bitterest pangs the human heart can bear. May I never experience the pain that results from becoming estranged from You. In Jesus' name. Amen.

'Giant Despair'

FOR READING & MEDITATION - ACTS 17:1-9

'They are all defying Caesar's decrees, saying that there is another king, one called Jesus.' (v7)

It is a well known fact that it is through our affections that we are most vulnerable, and some of the deepest pains human nature has to bear, east of Eden, come to us not through our enemies but through our friends.

John Bunyan, the famous tinker from Bedford, England, was imprisoned for unlicensed preaching. He languished in prison for much of the time between 1660 and 1672, being released after Charles II's Declaration of Indulgence, though he was jailed again briefly in 1675. While in prison he wrote several books, one of them being his spiritual autobiography entitled *Grace Abounding to the Chief of Sinners*, which he wrote in 1666. John Bunyan's enemies never shook him; it was his friends who caused him the greatest pain. When his enemies said to him, 'Promise not to preach and you can leave the prison today,' he replied, 'If you let me out today, I shall preach again tomorrow.' But when his friends visited him they took another line. 'Your concern about your conscience is fine,' they said, 'but what about your wife and children; who has to care for them? And what in particular, about Mary?' His daughter, Mary, was blind and doubly dependent on her father.*

FURTHER STUDY

Psa. 41:5-13;
Matt. 26:47-56;
Matt. 26:69-75

1. What relationship difficulties did the psalmist experience?

2. How did Jesus' friends let him down?

Some might think they were being reasonable, but not Bunyan. This kind of talk left him feeling very upset, and he says the shadow of Giant Despair seemed to hang around the cell for days. All this, however, sent him to his knees in passionate, persuasive prayer that God would keep him faithful. God did keep him faithful, and threw in *The Pilgrim's Progress* as well – the allegory based on Bunyan's spiritual life published in 1678.

Father, help me be faithful to You in all things, and grant that, like Bunyan, if it ever comes to a test of expediency, I might put You and Your interests first. In Jesus' name. Amen.

*You can read more about this in *John Bunyan: The People's Pilgrim* written by Peter Morden and published by CWR. Visit www.cwr.org.uk/store

Hating our loved ones?

FOR READING & MEDITATION - LUKE 14:25-35

'If anyone ... does not hate his father and mother, his wife and children ... he cannot be my disciple.' (v26)

We continue considering the fact that one of the sharpest pains our human nature must bear in this fallen world is disconnection in our relationships. And it is one of the great sadnesses of life that our friends and families sometimes cause that estrangement.

In the passage before us today Jesus tells us that if we are to be His disciples then we must be willing to hate our father, mother, wife, children, brothers, sisters, and our own lives also. What are we to make of this? Does Jesus really want us to *hate* our families and loved ones? Jesus here is using a vivid hyperbole (an exaggerated statement for the sake of emphasis), and what He means is that if we want to be His disciples then we must love Him more than our immediate family.

What a serious implication that word has for Christ's disciples. Our families, especially if they are non-Christians, believe they should come first in our lives, and when there is a clash of convictions and we are unwilling to compromise on something that is unbiblical the consequence may be disconnection. But if we want to be a disciple, then we must accept that He has the right to call the shots. What He says goes – even if our loved ones disagree.

Many great saints of the past knew the pain of estrangement in close relationships – people such as St Teresa of Avila, the educationalist St John Bosco, and the Indian preacher Sadhu Sundar Singh. However, when it came to a decision as to who would be first in their lives each of them chose Jesus. Blessed are those who, when faced with the disagreement of individuals to whom they looked for love, do not allow it to damage their faith in God.

FURTHER STUDY

Matt. 10:35-39;
Matt. 12:46-50;
Eph. 6:1-3;
1 Tim. 5:8

1. How does God regard our family?

2. How should we regard our family?

My Father and my God, I am a disciple and a follower of Your Son Jesus. Though this may involve me in separation from my family and friends, help me to put Him first, before every other affection. For Jesus' sake. Amen.

'Ask, man, ask'

FOR READING & MEDITATION - JAMES 1:1-8

'If any of you lacks wisdom, he should ask God ...
and it will be given to him.' (v5)

Dr E. Stanley Jones, one of my spiritual mentors, used to say, 'Christianity is the science of relating well to others in the spirit of Jesus Christ.' It is one thing when separation in our relationships is caused by us putting Jesus before all others for whom we feel affection, but quite another when we, because of our stubbornness, provoke a break in our relationships.

In a previous issue I have recounted how a man told me that his non-Christian neighbours and friends were persecuting him for the sake of the gospel. But after questioning him I discovered that his usual greeting to them was this: 'Hello, did you know that you are going to hell?' We must recognise the difference between estrangement resulting from our commitment to Jesus and that caused by our clumsiness and recklessness. Proverbs 11:30 says, 'He who wins souls is wise.' Though we cannot help it when others break their relationship with us because of our commitment to Jesus we must be careful that they are not alienated by our insensitivity and tactlessness. A friend of mine prays this prayer as soon as he opens his eyes in the morning: 'Lord, help me be wise in all my relationships this day and grant that I might not cause anyone to stumble because of a wrong word or action.' It's no wonder that this man is one of the greatest ambassadors for Jesus I know.

FURTHER STUDY

Matt. 7:7-12;
Col. 4:1-6

1. What is Jesus' promise?

2. How should we relate to those without faith?

My pastor in my youth was a very good spiritual director but sometimes when I presented him with a problem he would read me the verse which is at the top of this page and say, 'Have you asked God for wisdom over this issue?' If I answered 'No' he would then urge, 'Ask, man, ask.' This advice I now pass on to you.

Heavenly Father, my prayer is the same as that of the man I have just read about: 'Help me be wise in all my relationships this day and grant that I might not cause anyone to stumble because of a wrong word or action.' In Jesus' name. Amen.

'Let anyone who is **thirsty come to me** and drink.' John 7:37

Our schooldays and our teachers are remembered by many of us for our whole lives; they have such a powerful influence on us that they can shape who we are and, to a degree, what we do.

Will you help us equip men and women of character and send them out in their God given vocations as counsellors and teachers, to change lives and transform society for good? You can help us train many to be water carriers in a dry and thirsty land.

Please join us and help CWR to invest in building a generation of people who are strong in character and grounded in biblical truth.

Please fill in the 'Gift to CWR' section on the order form at the back of this publication, completing the Gift Aid declaration if appropriate.

'Loving well'

FOR READING & MEDITATION - ROMANS 5:1-11

'... God has poured out his love into our hearts by the Holy Spirit, whom he has given us.' (v5)

We spend one more day considering the fact that life in a fallen world sometimes brings the pain of disrupted relationships. At such times we must be careful that we do not allow the untrustworthiness of human emotions to damage our trust in God and our relationship with Him. And remember: if there is any estrangement between us and God then the cause is frequently on our side. To use the words of the old wayside pulpit poster, 'If God seems far away, guess who moved?'

One of the first lessons someone new in faith learns is that the closer our relationship with God the better we will be at handling our relationships with others. Why is this? Because people are erratic and sometimes, without any apparent reason, can turn against us. When this happens we need to remain secure in ourselves and continue loving in the way Jesus loves us. This is what I call *loving well* – continuing to love even in the face of possible rejection and hurt. It is almost impossible to do this if we rely on our human strength alone. No one likes to feel rejected and the instinctive human response is to reject the one who rejects us. The love of God, however, enables us to go on loving even though the love we give may not be reciprocated.

FURTHER STUDY

Luke 22:24-34; John 21:15-22

1. What did Jesus realise about His disciples?

2. How did Jesus love Peter well?

Estranged relationships may be one of the consequences of the Fall but they need not prevent us from loving well. The Almighty God has come to us in Christ and pours into our hearts something of His own love that enables us to go on loving even when, humanly speaking, we would give up on the person who has hurt us or withdrawn from us. Our love may fail – His love never.

Father, help me live closely to You so that I have the inner resources to love well. And if there are any broken relationships in my life help me attempt to repair them - beginning today. In Jesus' name. Amen.

Divine adequacy

FOR READING & MEDITATION - PSALM 112:1-10
'... his heart is steadfast, trusting in the LORD.' (v7)

We turn our attention to another potentially paralysing aspect of life which we have to deal with east of Eden – *anxiety and fear*. It is interesting that the very first negative emotion Adam confessed to after his declaration of independence was fear. When God said, 'Where are you?' he answered, 'I heard you in the garden, and I was *afraid*' (Gen. 3:9–10). Why was he afraid? Where did that fear come from? He had disconnected himself from God and, cut off from the source of his inner security, he felt inadequate to handle the situation that arose.

Underlying fear is a sense of being inadequate to meet the problems of life and relationships. This is a key – all else is merely a matter of dealing with the symptoms. Once the problem of inward inadequacy has been faced, fear drops away like a dead leaf. When we feel inadequate we don't know how to face life so we retreat into fear and anxiety. But when we learn to lean on God, then fear and anxiety are greatly reduced. Living as we do in a fallen world we may often find ourselves experiencing a sense of inadequacy to cope with the problems that arise. But there is a divine adequacy – a strength that comes through God's Holy Spirit. Drawing on His divine adequacy pushes fear and anxiety to the margin and beyond.

The early Christians demonstrated tremendous trust when facing fear. And it was not bravado. They had a quiet dignity and poise similar to that which Jesus possessed. Someone has commented, 'In the Gospels we hear Jesus exhorting His children not to be afraid. In the Acts we see them poised and unafraid.' This was not because there was nothing to fear but because they were unafraid of fear.

FURTHER STUDY

1 Sam. 10:17-24;
1 Sam. 17:32-37,
41-47

1. What was Saul's response to God's calling?

2. Contrast David's attitude to that of the giant Goliath.

Father, help me to overcome fears in my life. I know I can only do this as Your adequacy takes possession of me. I open every door in my heart to that adequacy today. Come in and fill me. In Jesus' name. Amen.

'Society of the Emancipated'

FOR READING & MEDITATION - ACTS 4:32-37

'With great power the apostles continued to testify to the resurrection of the Lord Jesus ...' (v33)

Yesterday we said that the early Christians had great trust in the face of fear. How did they achieve this when originally they were so full of fear?

Let's explore this some more. The disciples were afraid for their physical safety when they experienced a storm on the Sea of Galilee. They failed to realise that no storm could sink a boat that Jesus was in. Jesus said to them, 'You of little faith' (Matt. 8:26). On another occasion when they were on the lake they appeared to be afraid of the unknown. 'Jesus went out to them, walking on the lake. When the disciples saw him walking on the lake, they were terrified. "It's a ghost," they said, and cried out in fear. But Jesus immediately said to them: "Take courage! It is I. Don't be afraid"' (Matt. 14:25-27).

FURTHER STUDY

Acts 4:1-31

1. Why were the Sanhedrin astonished?

2. How did the disciples respond to their threats?

Were they afraid of their reputations? Well, certainly Jesus seemed to think they would experience this fear for He gave them this warning: 'If the head of the house has been called Beelzebub, how much more the members of his household!' (Matt. 10:25). They were afraid, too, of the spiritual world. At the time of Jesus' transfiguration we read this: 'When the disciples heard [a voice from the cloud] they fell face down to the ground, terrified. But Jesus came and touched them. "Get up," he said. "Don't be afraid"' (Matt. 17:6).

How did these disciples change so dramatically, for the Acts of the Apostles shows them to be afraid of nothing – life, death, opposition, the Roman authorities? They had been filled with adequacy, the adequacy of the Holy Spirit. Fear no longer paralysed them. They belonged to the 'Society of the Emancipated'. And the doors of that society are open to you and to me.

O Father, I am so thankful that I do not have to scurry here and there looking for remedies to overcome fear. In You I am safe no matter what happens. Burn this truth deeply into my spirit. In Jesus' name I pray. Amen.

Turning tests into testimonies

FOR READING & MEDITATION - LUKE 1:67-79

'... to rescue us from the hand of our enemies, and to enable us to serve him without fear ...' (v74)

No one knew better than Jesus how Adam and Eve's actions had affected human life in terms of anxiety and fear. In the Gospels we hear Him saying over and over again, 'Fear not.' One commentator claims that Jesus had more to say about fear than almost any other subject. I am not sure if this is so but one thing is certain: He was aware of a sense of fear in the hearts of men and women. So from the very first statement of the angel Gabriel to Mary – 'Do not be afraid' (Luke 1:30) – to Jesus' instruction after the resurrection – 'Do not be afraid. Go and tell my brothers to go to Galilee; there they will see me' (Matt. 28:10) – the life of Jesus was associated with freedom from fear.

The more dramatic change in the disciples came about after their experience of the Holy Spirit at Pentecost. Since fully embracing divine adequacy there really was nothing to fear because they could take something out of even the negative things they encountered. Threats? They turned them into opportunities for testimony. The more they were threatened, the more they testified. Prisons? They were either released by divine intervention or used the time in the service of the gospel, as did the apostle Paul when he wrote the epistles which we still read today. The future? They knew their future was assured and that they belonged to a kingdom that would last for ever.

A psychiatrist has said, 'A person who tastes fear tastes chaos; a person who tastes faith tastes cosmos.' The early Christians tasted cosmos – a new creation had come. They knew that God's creative strength within was adequate to transform every situation. When you know that – really know it – fear flows out.

FURTHER STUDY

Acts 16:16-34;
Phil. 1:12-21

1. How did the apostles turn a time of testing into a testimony?

2. What were the results of Paul's imprisonment?

Holy Spirit, by Your strength enable me to be creative, unafraid and prepared for anything that comes, knowing that with You and through You even opposition can become an opportunity. In Jesus' name. Amen.

His mind in ours

FOR READING & MEDITATION – 1 CORINTHIANS 2:6-16

'"For who has known the mind of the Lord that he may instruct him?" But we have the mind of Christ.' (v16)

A point that needs to be made when discussing fear and anxiety is that not all fears are harmful. Fear of being burned stops us putting our hand into a fire; fear of being hurt prevents us from rushing across a busy road. Unhappily, however, fear does not only have a beneficent role. Fear, as the Authorised Version of the Bible tells us, has *torment* (1 John 4:18). It can paralyse us and prevent us moving forward in life.

How is it that Jesus was able to live free from fear's paralysing power? It is important to remember that He too lived in this fallen world. One commentator says, 'The whole meaning of God taking our flesh is that we should learn what God is like and how the life of God can be lived in our world.' The world into which Jesus came was, and still is, a world encompassing sickness and suffering, malice and hate, treachery and deceitfulness. There were many things of which He could have been afraid. His secret was that He had such complete trust in His Father's love and power that He could go through life free from the paralysis of fear. His fearlessness was rooted in His complete confidence that His Father loved Him and would not allow anything to happen to Him unless it accorded with His purposes.

FURTHER STUDY

Exod. 14:10-31;
Prov. 29:25

1. Contrast the attitudes of Moses and the Israelites.

2. What may trap and restrict us?

Assured of that, what would He fear? Infinite wisdom and infinite love were over and behind everything. He knew that the most diabolical machinations of evil were powerless against the throne of God. Jesus could face the darkest probabilities and not be afraid. Filled with trust and love, His mind had no fissures in which fear could hide. And because His mind is in us, as our text for today tells us, neither need we.

Father, help me to keep ever before me this simple fact that whatever You allow into my life will work for good to me. Impress this thought so deeply into my spirit that it will stay with me at all times. In Jesus' name. Amen.

Think – and be free

FOR READING & MEDITATION – 1 JOHN 4:7-21

'There is no fear in love. But perfect love drives out fear, because
fear has to do with punishment.' (v18)

We are discovering, I trust, that one way to deal with the problem of fear and anxiety is to be assured of the fact that our loving heavenly Father will never allow anything to happen in our life unless it can be ultimately turned to good. Today's text has, I believe, done more to help me deal with fear and anxiety in my own life than any other verse in Scripture. Look at the words again: 'There is no fear in love.' But what does that really mean?

Well, think about it like this: we are never afraid of those whom we know love us, and love us deeply. We trust ourselves in their hands and, because we are convinced of their love, we are not afraid of the way they behave towards us. Even when we cannot understand the purpose of their actions – even if they may appear not to be benevolent – we nevertheless give them the benefit of the doubt. Because they love us we know they will not do anything to harm us. Now lift what is true in our human relationships to the level of our relationship with God. Listen to what the text says once more: 'Perfect love drives out fear.' *Perfect* love, notice that. The love that God has for us is free from any taint of imperfection. It is unconditional, unchanging, and will never be withdrawn.

The more we allow our minds to dwell on the fact that we are loved the more likely it is that our emotions will get the message. What we think about affects the way we feel, and the way we feel affects the way we act. So think about how much you are loved. Think about it constantly. Dwell on the fact until it transforms your emotions. This is the only remedy for fear and anxiety that works. I know, because it works for me.

FURTHER STUDY

Matt. 25:14-27;
Rom. 8:28-39

1. How may our potential be released or restricted?

2. Of what was Paul convinced?

Father, forgive me if I have simply been wishing that fear and anxiety would disappear from my life. Now I see that I have a part to play in the matter too. Help me think constantly about Your undying love for me. In Jesus' name. Amen.

FOR READING & MEDITATION - PSALM 1:1-6

'But his delight is in the law of the LORD, and on his law he meditates day and night.' (v2)

Now we move on to consider yet another matter which we have to deal with as a result of the Fall – *inner unrest*. Though many are disinclined to admit to it, there is a sense of unease and dissatisfaction in the heart of every man and woman, irrespective of their race, creed, culture or colour. At the core of every person's being there is a hunger and thirst for something, which remains there even after they have tasted the finest pleasures the world can give. Why is this?

FURTHER STUDY

Psa. 37:1-7;
Psa. 119:9-24

1. How can we find fulfilment?

2. What made the psalmist happy?

The reason, I believe, is that when God created Adam and Eve in His image He designed them first and foremost for a relationship with Himself. This means in practical terms that they could not function effectively or feel completely at peace within themselves outside of a relationship with Him. This disconnection with God which took place in Eden resulted, as we saw, in the image of God within them becoming fractured and marred: marred but not destroyed. All who come from Adam and Eve are image-bearers still, and though we do not reflect God in the way He originally intended, there is within us all an innate sense that we will never be at ease with ourselves until we are once again at ease with God.

An atheist, in a statement I thought was so open and honest, once said to me, 'I am intellectually convinced there is no God, but there are times when I wish my convictions were not so firm so that I could let my heart be free to pursue the desire for transcendence which it seems to possess.' St Augustine's great prayer, which is often quoted, best sums it up: 'You have made us for Yourself, and our hearts are restless until they find their rest in You.'

Heavenly Father, my prayer today is for the multitudes who deep down in their hearts long to know You yet deny the very idea of Your existence. Help them come to know You as I have come to know You. In Jesus' name. Amen.

Hungry and thirsty: for what?

FOR READING & MEDITATION – ECCLESIASTES 3:1-15

'He has also set eternity in the hearts of men ...' (v11)

Following on from what we said yesterday about there being unrest in the heart of everyone descended from Adam, let me retell this legend from the Western Isles of Scotland which helps to illustrate the issue.

One day a sea king longed for the company of a human being. A little while later, in his cavern under the sea, he heard a cry – a faint human cry. When he rose to the surface he discovered a child in a boat that was drifting. Just as he was about to make for the little vessel and take the child, a rescue party intervened and he missed his prize. But, according to the legend, as the rescue party headed away the sea king cupped his hands and threw into the heart of the child a little drop of the sea. As he became submerged once again he said to himself, 'That child is mine. When he grows the sea will call him and he will come home to me at last.'

This is only a story, of course, but how wonderfully it illustrates the truth of today's text. God put into the hearts of Adam and Eve a longing for Himself, and though their sin damaged their personalities, and that damage was passed on to the whole human race, the longings are still there – deep and ineradicable. Millions of men and women cannot understand it. They just know that at times – perhaps when they gaze up at the stars at night or when they are alone – they sense that there are longings within them for something inexplicable.

I wonder, are any of you reading these lines hungering and thirsting for something you cannot identify? Could it be that you have never opened your heart to God and His Son Jesus Christ? If you have not already done this, do so now I beg you. Pray this prayer and turn your life over to Him.

FURTHER STUDY

Gen. 50:22-26;
Josh. 24:32;
Heb. 11:8-16

1. What was Joseph's longing?

2. What did Abraham thirst for?

Heavenly Father, I see that You, and You alone, can truly satisfy my soul. I ask forgiveness for every sin I have ever committed. Cleanse me and make me a Christian. Save me now. In Jesus' name. Amen.

One Bible. One Year.
Together.

Consider this: reading the Bible daily, knowing that your church are reading the same words with you. If you struggle to read the Bible every day, if you don't quite understand what a passage means or how it relates to you – you're surrounded by people who will understand and listen. Reading the Bible together strengthens relationships, deepens knowledge and most importantly establishes the entire church in God's Word.

'One Bible. One Year. Together.' is about putting God's Word back at the centre of our lives. It's the beginning of the greatest journey of all: our daily walk with God. Read more than the usual scriptures you turn to; read the entire Bible in a year. There's so much more to God for us to discover together.

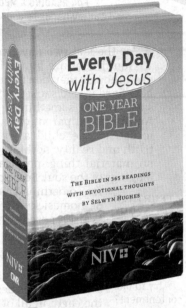

The new edition of *Every Day with Jesus One Year Bible* (NIV 2011) offers:
- 365 daily selections from the Old Testament, New Testament, Psalms and Proverbs
- life-related devotional notes by Selwyn Hughes that tie directly into the scriptures
- prayers and notes for further study.

Also available in eBook/Kindle versions

FREE Welcome Pack

When your church registers, we will send you a FREE Welcome Pack which contains a range of resources to help you promote 'One Bible. One Year. Together' to your whole church. This includes posters, invitation cards and information about bulk purchase offers. All those who take part will also receive a FREE *Every Day with Jesus* notebook and bookmark with their Bible.*

To register visit **www.cwr.org.uk/store** or call 01252 784 710. Place your order before 30th November for a guaranteed start on 1 January.

*while stocks last

'I don't know what I want'

FOR READING & MEDITATION – PSALM 143:1-12

'I spread out my hands to you; my soul thirsts for you like a parched land.' (v6)

For the last two days we have touched on the fact that multitudes are hungering and thirsting for something, even though they don't know what it is. Any parent knows how hard it is to satisfy a child who comes to the table and says, 'I want something ... but I don't know what I want.' An insightful parent or carer can usually find something to satisfy the child after such a vague request, but in truth and reality, nothing on this planet – no relationship, no material thing, no pleasure – can satisfy the deepest longings of the soul. Some people say that this longing in us for something that earth cannot satisfy is a kind of homesickness in the soul. The poet William Watson posed this question in one of his poems:

FURTHER STUDY

Eccl. 2:1-23;
Eccl. 12:13

1. How did Solomon try to find contentment?

2. What was his conclusion?

In this house with starry dome
Shall I never feel at home?

Never! Since Adam was made out of the earth and we are his descendants there is something of the earth in all of us. However, there are longings in us that earth cannot satisfy. Earth seems to satisfy the animals and the birds. They eat their fill and they seem to be content. But it cannot satisfy us.

The Israelite people were led to understand this during their 40-year journey through the desert (Deut. 8:3). Jesus used these same words to remind us that we cannot live by bread alone (Matt. 4:4). We have longings that cause us to cry out for a relationship with God. How sad it is to realise that multitudes will die today ignorant of the fact that their deepest longings, which earth could not satisfy, could have been satisfied in a relationship with God and His Son Jesus Christ.

O Father, I cannot thank You enough for the fact that I will not die in ignorance of this fact. Knowing You as I do meets and fills my deepest longings. And I exult in the assurance that this is not only for time but for eternity too. Amen.

FOR READING & MEDITATION – JOHN 7:37-44

'... Jesus stood and said in a loud voice, "If anyone is thirsty,
let him come to me and drink."' (v37)

A leader tells of a charming young woman who informed him that she did not have a care in the world. She was happily married, her children were growing up nicely and she had plenty of friends. But then she added, 'I'm half ashamed to admit that despite that I'm still wanting something I can't clearly define. Sometimes I think it is just a sense of peace, and sometimes I think it is a bigger purpose in life, and sometimes I fancy I need to see more plainly the meaning of things … and sometimes I wonder if it is *just God*.'

This inner unrest which all of us experience east of Eden is not something we have to live with. God has made it possible for this ache in our soul to be satisfied. It is one of the tasks of every Christian community to make the hunger of the soul clear to people, and any church that does not do this is failing in its responsibility. In this respect the human heart is an ally, for the homesickness felt by the soul is there because everyone has been built for a relationship with God. A major task of the Church is to focus on this and show people how their thirst can be quenched.

FURTHER STUDY

Acts 17:16-34

1. How did the Athenians show inner unrest?

2. How did Paul focus on and clarify their unrest?

Our passage for today tells how, centuries ago, Jesus stood and said in a loud voice, 'If anyone is thirsty, let him come to me and drink.' Notice the words 'in a loud voice'. Why the *loud* voice? Why such passion and concern? While Jesus watched the pageantry of the Feast of Tabernacles His soul would have been moved within Him as He contemplated the fact that rituals could never satisfy the deep thirsts and longings of the soul. He alone is the answer to the soul's greatest need. Jesus is crying out still. How sad that many cannot hear and respond to His voice.

O Father, speak with a loud voice into the hearts of men and women all over the world today. Unstop their deaf ears. Save them heavenly Father. In Jesus' name I ask it. Amen.

'Tossed to His breast'

FOR READING & MEDITATION - JOHN 6:25-40

'Jesus declared, "... He who comes to me will never go hungry, and he who believes in me will never be thirsty."' (v35)

We spend another day reflecting on the thought that one of the issues we have to deal with as a result of the Fall is that of inner unrest when actually it is a blessing in disguise. If earth could satisfy us then we would not seek God. George Herbert, in a rather quaint poem, made the point that if the revelation of God's goodness fails to lead men and women to Him then perhaps the weariness they experience as a result of trying to find satisfaction in things outside of Him might do so. Speaking on behalf of the Father he wrote, 'If goodness lead him not, yet weariness may toss him to My breast.' How many people will we meet in heaven, I wonder, who will testify to the fact that their efforts to find peace and joy in something other than Christ brought about a weariness that at last caused them to turn to Him?

FURTHER STUDY

Psa. 63:1-11;
Psa. 84:1-12

1. Identify the psalmist's feelings.

2. Where would the psalmist find satisfaction?

The weariness that came from trying to find satisfaction for the ache in my soul outside of Christ was what finally led me to Him. It tossed me to His breast. One of my favourite hymns, and the one the congregation was singing the night I came to know Jesus Christ, puts it most beautifully:

I heard the voice of Jesus say: Come unto Me and rest;
Lay down, thou weary one, lay down thy head upon My breast!
I came to Jesus as I was, weary, and worn, and sad;
I found in Him a resting-place, and He has made me glad.

There is a thirst in the soul which no water on earth can satisfy; a hunger unmet except by the manna which comes down from heaven. Jesus alone is the answer.

Father, once more I want to offer You my thanks for leading me from inner unrest to inner rest. What no one else could do for me You have done. You satisfy my deepest longings. All honour and glory be to Your name for ever. Amen.

An internal disease

FOR READING & MEDITATION – ROMANS 7:7-25

'What a wretched man I am! Who will rescue me from this
body of death?' (v24)

As we continue looking at some of the hard things we
are called to bear east of Eden we come to the issue of
our *fallen human nature*. Theologians have a term for the
pervasive effect of sin – 'total depravity'. My dictionary
defines 'depravity' in this way: 'corrupt state of moral
character, extreme wickedness, the hereditary tendency
of man towards sin'. The truth is that every one of us has
a bias towards ungodliness and independence – a legacy
passed on to us by the first human pair.

It's important to understand that this is an *internal*
disease. Generally people don't appear to be
depraved or corrupt and bankrupt because most
of us do a masterful job at covering it up. But
never doubt that underneath, deep down inside,
there is this corruption that eats away at us,
polluting our thoughts, our words, our actions,
our relationships and even our will.

**FURTHER
STUDY**

Jer. 17:5-9;
Rom. 1:18-32

1. What is the
nature of the
human heart?

A Scottish preacher once confided in a private
moment to a colleague, 'If you could see into my
heart you would spit in my face.' Contemplating
the evil that is in the world, and realising that it
stems from deep within, one poet expressed his
thoughts in these poignant words:

2. How does our
fallen nature
influence us?

I know a bosom which within
Contains the world's sad counterpart,
'Tis here – the reign of death and sin.
O God, evangelise my heart!

We hear the same cry from the apostle Paul in the
passage before us today. He knew that if he was going to
have control over the inner corruption then the answer lay
in part outside of himself.

**Heavenly Father, I see that corruption is so deeply ingrained
in me that I am powerless to clean up my own act. But I see
also that You have a plan to evangelise my heart. For that I am
eternally grateful. Amen.**

Murder in our heart?

FOR READING & MEDITATION - GENESIS 5:1-5

'When Adam had lived 130 years, he had a son in his own likeness, in his own image ...' (v3)

Yesterday we said that every one of us has within a legacy passed on to us by the first human pair. Human corruption is one of the unfortunate and devastating effects of the Fall. Once Adam and Eve sinned their nature became corrupted, but their corruption was not confined to them; they passed it on to their descendants.

Look again at these words: 'When God created man, he made him in the likeness of God' (v1). Now listen to this: 'When Adam had lived 130 years, he had a son in his own likeness, in his own image; and he named him Seth.' Can you see what is being said here? 'When God created man, he made him in the likeness of God.' That's how God made Adam – in His own likeness. But then we read, 'When Adam had lived 130 years, he had a son *in his own likeness*.' God created Adam and Eve in *His* likeness; Adam and Eve created Seth in *their* likeness. Without exception, every person who has ever lived and will ever live has within them this bias towards ungodliness.

FURTHER STUDY

Matt. 5:21-30;
Matt. 15:10-20;
1 John 3:11-18

1. What did Jesus explain?

2. How can we be like Cain?

Adam and Eve's firstborn was Cain who, as you know, killed his brother Abel (Gen. 4:1-8). Why? Because his thinking was corrupted. Emotionally he was intensely jealous. Spiritually he was dead. You might think to yourself: what a terrible man Cain must have been. But remember: we too are corrupted. In our hearts there is potentially the same murderous nature. You may not stab someone with a hunting knife but have you stabbed someone with your tongue? We can cut into someone's life with our thoughts or even our looks. How sad that we can cluck our tongues at the thought of Cain murdering his brother Abel and yet, perhaps, be guilty of entertaining murderous thoughts in our own hearts.

Heavenly Father, there is something within me that is unwilling to acknowledge my ungodliness. Please help me because I see that until I acknowledge this I cannot be whole. In Jesus' name. Amen.

A congenital disease

FOR READING & MEDITATION - JAMES 1:9-18

'... each one is tempted when, by his own evil desire,
he is dragged away and enticed.' (v14)

We are seeing that the devastating results of the Fall have spread throughout the whole human race. They not only passed from Adam and Eve's generation into the next but continued on into the next ... and the next ... and they are still with us here today – a long way from Eden. Corruption is in you and it's in me. Some theologians have likened it to a congenital disease. The disease is there from birth. And it is disfiguring; it mars the image of God in us so that the Father cannot see His reflection in us. But how does our depraved nature reveal itself? Here are some of its effects.

Greed and lust is one outcome. Our fallen human nature has some powerful instinctive drives. However, God has said that we need not passively give way to them but rather build a life in which God regulates our appetite. In some people all troubles are minor in comparison with their battle with greed and lust. When tempted where are men and women able to find the strength to resist these fierce drives? Only in Christ. He not only conducts the moral tests on our soul but He gives us the grace to pass them.

Another effect of our inner depravity is a bad or short temper. People who are bad tempered are touchy; they flare up at the least provocation and sometimes no provocation at all. Bad-tempered people think others are to blame for setting them off; they fail to see that the problem is often theirs. And it's no good excusing ourselves by saying, 'It's my nature to be bad tempered.' Jesus has given us a new nature, a nature that overcomes our old nature and provides us with new purity, power and grace. You can trust God to allow His new nature to overcome your old nature. Turn to Him today.

FURTHER STUDY

Eph. 2:1-4;
Eph. 4:17-32

1. What are the desires and thoughts of a sinful nature?

2. Contrast the old and new natures.

Heavenly Father, I know I have a fight on my hands but help me realise that Your power enables me to overcome all inner conflicts. Help me to lay hold on that power. In Jesus' name. Amen.

More effects of corruption

FOR READING & MEDITATION - GALATIANS 5:16-26

'The acts of the sinful nature are obvious: sexual immorality,
impurity and debauchery ...' (v19)

Another outcome of our fallen human nature is pride. Although all sin is dangerous, some theologians view pride as the most deadly of the so-called 'seven deadly sins'. There is little doubt in my mind that they are right. St Augustine held the view that obstinate pride was the unpardonable sin itself.

Fallen human nature is shot through with pride, and the real germ of this disease is that it puts self in the centre. It struts and shouts and brags. It strikes an attitude of I ... I ... I, and it makes the puffed up ego the centre of everything.

FURTHER STUDY

Luke 18:9-14;
Eph. 5:1-21

1. What may be a problem of religious people?

2. How relevant is Paul's writing in the 21st Century?

Lust requires a passive mind in which to flourish. Pride can even propagate itself in the soil of virtue. For instance, we can give generously to good causes and be proud of our giving. We can pray eloquently and be proud of our praying. If Christ is to live in us then pride has to die in us.

There are many other effects of our fallen human nature but let me mention just one more – jealousy. Have you noticed how sometimes it is much easier to sympathise with our friends in their sorrows than be happy for them in their successes? Jealousy does not leap a chasm; it gets into the cracks. By that I mean we are rarely jealous of those who far outshine us. Rather, we are jealous of those we regard as being our equal, who move in our circle but have outstripped us. Can Jesus help us overcome this corruption in our nature, this depravity in our soul? Yes, but again He can do so only if we bring all we are to Him, ask His forgiveness for our wrongdoing and drink deeply of His grace and strength. He can take from us if we ask Him (and let Him) the eagerness for human praise which is the cause of so much jealousy.

Lord Jesus Christ, so live in me I pray that everything that is not of You will die in me. Take from me all that is displeasing to You and replace it with all that is pleasing to You. For Your own dear name's sake. Amen.

'Yield not to temptation'

FOR READING & MEDITATION - ROMANS 6:15-23

'... when you offer yourselves to someone to obey him as slaves,
you are slaves to the one whom you obey ...' (v16)

The disease of depravity is so invasive that only the Divine Physician is fully equal to dealing with it. Yesterday I said that Jesus is able to help us curb the desires that come from our corrupt nature, but there are things we must do as well. We will only make progress in overcoming our own nature when we realise that we cannot trust it.

Heed this word of counsel: never allow yourself to get into a situation where your nature will take charge. If you are struggling with lust when you are around others then keep away from situations in which you know you might give way to temptation. If you play with fire it won't be long before you get burnt. And it won't be anyone's fault except yours. It is tremendously important to keep a safe distance whenever you sense the temptation to become involved in something unhelpful to you. In today's world God's original design is being compromised. If you are sleeping with your girlfriend or boyfriend then you are not living with the best that God has for you. Stop doing it. You may need to face the consequences, ask for God's forgiveness, and get back on track spiritually.

FURTHER STUDY

Gen. 39:1-12;
2 Tim. 2:20-22

1. How did Joseph avoid temptation?

2. How should Timothy avoid evil desires?

How could a man as godly as David fall as he did with Bathsheba? And how could he be responsible for sending her husband Uriah to his death on the battlefield? I will tell you. He gave in to his carnal nature. As lust played its sweet song the king of Israel danced to its music. Lust didn't simply rise up and overtake him. He passively gave way to it and then it was not long before he added murder to the sin of adultery. He was responsible for what he did, just as you and I are every time we yield to a temptation. We sin because we want to – never forget that.

Gracious and loving heavenly Father, help me understand that no sin can overtake me unless I willingly yield to it. Help me say 'No' to every temptation and yield my heart only to You. In Jesus' name. Amen.

FOR READING & MEDITATION – JOB 5:1-7

'Yet man is born to trouble as surely as sparks fly upward.' (v7)

Yet another distressing and disturbing aspect of life we have to deal with east of Eden is that of *unmerited suffering*. The text before us today reminds us that 'Man is born to trouble as surely as sparks fly upward'. There are few of us, I imagine, who have not had cause to agree with the truth of those words.*

Regular readers may remember my references to a another observer of the human condition who wrote,

My son, the world is dark with griefs, and graves,
So dark that men cry out against the heavens.

FURTHER STUDY

Job 2:1-10;
Luke 16:19-31

1. Contrast the attitudes of Job and his wife.

2. Why was the rich man's attitude to life wrong?

I suppose there is nothing that makes men and women 'cry out against the heavens' so much as the anguish caused by unmerited suffering. Contrasting different human responses to life events, philosopher Horace Walpole said, 'To those who *think*, life is a comedy; to those who *feel*, life is a tragedy.' And as most of us will, at times, focus on our feelings, most of us will, at times, see life as a tragedy. Mercifully God has not left us to face this great problem of unmerited suffering on our own.

Before we consider a biblical worldview of this problem, however, let's look at ways in which the world seeks to deal with this great predicament. One way is that of Stoicism – accepting the fact of suffering and steeling yourself against it. Stoicism in its purest form seeks to become indifferent to pleasure or pain and attempts to achieve self-control through fortitude or austerity. Stoicism is not an answer to unmerited suffering but a defence against it. In my view, it somewhat lacks integrity, as integrity requires that whatever is true has to be faced and felt.

O Father, help me to always be a person of integrity and to be willing to acknowledge matters rather than duck into defences. With You I can face anything that comes. I am so grateful. In Jesus' name. Amen.

*Michael Baughen writes about this issue in *The One Big Question: The God of love in a world of suffering* published by CWR. Visit www.cwr.org.uk/store

More ways of the world

FOR READING & MEDITATION – JOHN 16:17-33

'In this world you will have trouble. But take heart! I have overcome the world.' (v33)

Omar Khayyam, the Persian poet, looked upon this world with all its misery and pain and his reaction to it was this:

> To grasp this sorry scheme of things entire …
> Shatter it to bits – and then remould it to
> my heart's desire.

His answer was different from that of Stoicism; it was to remake the world with the possibility of suffering left out. Sadly, as that cannot be done we need to consider the poet's words as expressing idealism and not grounded in reality. They make good poetry but are of no help to those who are in the midst of deep suffering.

Many people go about the business of dealing with unmerited suffering by accepting that it is inevitable and always anticipating it. 'This type of mentality,' says one commentator, 'tries to cheat the jinx by always expecting it.' It argues, 'I was not caught unawares … I knew it would come.' This is the way of disillusioned cynicism.

Others cope with unmerited suffering by lapsing into self-pity, almost getting pleasure out of feeling sorry for themselves. The classic Hindu attitude to suffering is to see it as resulting from choices from a previous birth. Many Muslims deal with the problem by believing that all that happens is God's will. Accept suffering as the will of God, they say, and submit to it.

Christian Science dismisses suffering and sickness as being unreal. They exist only in our mind, they claim. Any system that takes your attention off the grim facts of life creates a shallow optimism that is almost certainly doomed to turn into pessimism.

FURTHER STUDY

Eccl. 5:8-17;
John 9:1-7

1. What was the attitude of the teacher?

2. What was the disciples' attitude to suffering?

Heavenly Father, I see a society that really has no effective answers to this problem of unmerited suffering. My heart is open to Your answers. Teach me Your way dear Lord. Amen.

Where suffering comes from

FOR READING & MEDITATION - LUKE 21:5-19

'There will be great earthquakes, famines and pestilences in various places, and fearful events ...' (v11)

Evil, it has been said, is of two kinds – one which arises from within and the other which comes from without. We can understand how we come to suffer within when we make wrong and poor choices but why should we suffer when we have done nothing to deserve it? Why should evil and suffering come upon us from without? Once again we need to understand that the world is under a curse and, whether we like it or not – indeed, whether we believe it or not – suffering is part of what we experience living as we do east of Eden.

FURTHER STUDY

Luke 13:1-5;
1 John 5:1-5

1. What did Jesus explain about suffering?

2. How can we overcome?

In today's reading Jesus identifies a number of forms of suffering and does, in fact, give us a summary of the routes along which suffering can come. Jesus is essentially talking of the signs of the end of the age, but some of these troubles have been with us from the beginning of time. Suffering comes, says Jesus, from the mental and spiritual confusion in regard to the destructive things of life; from wars; from physical calamities such as earthquakes, floods, fire, storm; from toxicity that creeps into our foods, into the air we breathe; from economic distress caused by famines; from the fact that society opposes us and persecutes us because we depart from its spirit and standards; from the oppression that comes from religious and secular authorities; from difficulties in the home and, of course, from our association with Jesus Himself.

This is not a complete list of the ways in which suffering can come but it's more than enough! It's so important not to forget that Jesus is with us in all our suffering. He will never leave us or forsake us. Remember He said, 'Take heart! I have overcome the world' (John 16:33).

Father, I see that even though I am not exempt from suffering, because I am Your child I most certainly cannot be exempted from being a recipient of Your grace. And for that I am deeply thankful. Amen.

Are Christians spared?

FOR READING & MEDITATION – HEBREWS 11:32-40

'Some faced jeers and flogging, while still others were chained
and put in prison.' (v36)

It is clear from the passage before us now that God's people are not always spared from suffering. It is true that there have been times when God has miraculously preserved people from torment and anguish, for example, Shadrach, Meshach and Abednego (Dan. 3). It is also true that God heals people of disease and afflictions. I wouldn't be writing this today if that were not the case. But it is not always so. If God's people were saved from suffering then people would crowd into our churches and become Christians as a kind of divine insurance policy. However, that is not the way God extends His Church. So how do the people of God deal with suffering whether it is physical, mental, or spiritual? By what strategy do Christians maintain their faith?

FURTHER STUDY

2 Cor. 11:18-33;
2 Cor. 12:7-10

1. How did Paul suffer?

2. What answer did he find in his sufferings?

Paul's example is a good one for us to follow. To read slowly and imaginatively his catalogue of bitter experiences in 2 Corinthians 11 and how he dealt with them is to be lost in wonder and admiration. Toils, imprisonments, beatings, stonings, shipwrecks, treachery, hunger, thirst, coldness, nakedness – he knew them all; and on top of this there was his daily concern for the churches. In the following chapter Paul tells us that he 'delighted' in the troubles that came to him (2 Cor. 12:10). Delighted? I would have thought he might have used a word other than 'delighted'. How can one 'delight' in suffering?

The answer, in part, is that he experienced the grace of God in his weakness and found that the more deprivations he went through the more God's strength flowed into him. Finding God in a deeper way is the key. Nothing can prevent Him from coming to us.

Gracious Father, I rejoice that there are no obstacles, no barriers and no difficulties that cannot be overcome because You draw near to me in times of difficulty. Blessed be Your holy name for ever. Amen.

Have it Your own way, Father

FOR READING & MEDITATION - JOB 1:1-22

'The LORD gave and the LORD has taken away; may the name of the LORD be praised.' (v21)

Scripture shows that those who were called to suffer were enabled to do so because they did not put undue emphasis on the difference between what God does and what He permits. They found God even in what He allowed. Because the world belongs to God they saw Him as taking responsibility for whatever happens. If anything was devoid of good they believed God would not permit it.

Job did not regard his sufferings as coming from the Sabeans, or the Chaldeans, or even 'from natural causes'. He took them from God. 'The LORD gave,' he said, 'and the LORD has taken away.' The psalmist locked into the same truth. 'All your waves and breakers have swept over me,' he said (Psa. 42:7). Somewhere at the heart of bitter experiences, the psalmist implies, there is a loving purpose at work. They were God's waves and God's breakers.

FURTHER STUDY

Gen. 50:15-21;
John 12:23-33;
John 16:20-22

1. How did Jesus view His time of suffering?

2. Why may a time of sorrow be positive?

Then there is the example of the Saviour Himself. Every Christian is familiar with what happened in Gethsemane. There Jesus prayed, 'My Father, if it is possible, may this cup be taken from me' (Matt. 26:39). Later He said, 'Shall I not drink the cup the Father has given me?' (John 18:11). *The contents of any cup can be transformed when we see that the hand holding it is that of the Father.* It is as if Jesus said, 'If this is what My Father wants Me to do then I will do it. I will not take it from Judas, Pilate, Caiaphas or the people. I will take it only from My Father.'

An elderly woman who experienced much suffering resolved any difference between her and God by saying, 'Have it Your own way, Father.' The secret of triumphing over suffering is to accept that God never allows anything to happen to us without providing the strength to handle it.

O Father, when suffering comes help me not to put undue emphasis on the difference between what You do and what You permit. And may I also never lose sight of the fact that You allow only what You can use. In Jesus' name. Amen.

PAYMENT DETAILS

☐ I enclose a cheque/PO made payable to CWR for the amount of: **£**

☐ Please charge my credit/debit card.

Cardholder's name (in BLOCK CAPITALS)

Card No.

Expires end

Security Code

GIFT TO CWR ☐ Please send me an acknowledgement of my gift   **C**

GIFT AID (YOUR HOME ADDRESS REQUIRED, SEE OVERLEAF)

giftaid it

I am a UK taxpayer and want CWR to reclaim the tax on all my donations for the four years prior to this year **and on** all donations I make from the date of this Gift Aid declaration until further notice.*

Taxpayer's Full Name (in BLOCK CAPITALS)

Signature _____ **Date** _____

*I understand I must pay an amount of Income/Capital Gains Tax at least equal to the tax the charity reclaims in the tax year.

GRAND TOTAL (Total of A, B, & C)

SUBSCRIPTIONS BY DIRECT DEBIT (UK BANK ACCOUNT HOLDERS ONLY)

Subscriptions cost £15.95 (except *Mettle*: £14.50) for one year for delivery within the UK. Please tick relevant boxes and fill in the form

☐ *Every Day with Jesus* (1yr, 6 issues)
☐ Large Print *Every Day with Jesus* (1yr, 6 issues)
☐ *Inspiring Women Every Day* (1yr, 6 issues)
☐ *Life Every Day* (Jeff Lucas) (1yr, 6 issues)

☐ *Cover to Cover Every Day* (1yr, 6 issues)
☐ *Mettle*: 14-18s (1yr, 3 issues)
☐ *YP's*: 11-15s (1yr, 6 issues)
☐ *Topz*: 7-11s (1yr, 6 issues)

Issue to commence
☐ Jan/Feb ☐ Jul/Aug
☐ Mar/Apr ☐ Sep/Oct
☐ May/Jun ☐ Nov/Dec

CWR

Instruction to your Bank or
Building Society to pay by Direct Debit

DIRECT Debit

Please fill in the form and send to: CWR, Waverley Abbey House, Waverley Lane, Farnham, Surrey GU9 8EP

Name and full postal address of your Bank or Building Society

To: The Manager _____ Bank/Building Society

Address

Postcode

Name(s) of Account Holder(s)

Branch Sort Code

Bank/Building Society account number

Originator's Identification Number

| 4 | 2 | 0 | 4 | 8 | 7 |

Reference

Instruction to your Bank or Building Society

Please pay CWR Direct Debits from the account detailed in this Instruction subject to the safeguards assured by the Direct Debit Guarantee.
I understand that this Instruction may remain with CWR and, if so, details will be passed electronically to my Bank/Building Society.

Signature(s)

Date

Banks and Building Societies may not accept Direct Debit Instructions for some types of account

ORDER FORM

4 EASY WAYS TO ORDER:

1. Phone in your credit card order: **01252 784710** (Mon-Fri, 9.30am - 5pm)

2. Visit our Online Store at **www.cwr.org.uk/store**

3. Send this form together with your payment to:
   CWR, Waverley Abbey House, Waverley Lane, Farnham, Surrey GU9 8EP

4. Visit your local Christian bookshop

r a list of our National Distributors, who supply countries outside the UK, visit www.cwr.org.uk/distributors

YOUR DETAILS (REQUIRED FOR ORDERS AND DONATIONS)

Name:	CWR ID No. (if known):
Home Address:	
	Postcode:
Telephone No. (for queries):	Email:

PUBLICATIONS

TITLE	QTY	PRICE	TOTAL
		Total publications	

All CWR adult Bible-reading notes are also available in ebook and email subscription format.
Visit **www.cwr.org.uk** for further information.

UK p&p: up to £24.99 = **£2.99**; £25.00 and over = **FREE**
Elsewhere p&p: up to £10 = **£4.95**; £10.01 - £50 = **£6.95**; £50.01 - £99.99 = **£10**; £100 and over = **£30**

Please allow 14 days for delivery   **Total publications and p&p A** | |

SUBSCRIPTIONS* (NON DIRECT DEBIT)

	QTY	PRICE (INCLUDING P&P)			TOTAL
		UK	Europe	Elsewhere	
Every Day with Jesus (1yr, 6 issues)		£15.95	£19.95	Please contact nearest National Distributor or CWR direct	
Large Print *Every Day with Jesus* (1yr, 6 issues)		£15.95	£19.95		
Inspiring Women Every Day (1yr, 6 issues)		£15.95	£19.95		
Life Every Day (Jeff Lucas) (1yr, 6 issues)		£15.95	£19.95		
Cover to Cover Every Day (1yr, 6 issues)		£15.95	£19.95		
Mettle: 14-18s (1yr, 3 issues)		£14.50	£16.60		
YP's: 11-15s (1yr, 6 issues)		£15.95	£19.95		
Topz: 7-11s (1yr, 6 issues)		£15.95	£19.95		
Total Subscriptions (Subscription prices already include postage and packing) **B**					

lease circle which bimonthly issue you would like your subscription to commence from:
an/Feb Mar/Apr May/Jun Jul/Aug Sep/Oct Nov/Dec

Only use this section for subscriptions paid for by credit/debit card or
cheque. For Direct Debit subscriptions see overleaf.

CONTINUED OVERLEAF >>

Seeing the glory of God

FOR READING & MEDITATION - ACTS 7:54-60

'"Look," he said, "I see heaven open and the Son of Man standing at the right hand of God."' (v56)

On this the last day of considering the theme 'east of Eden' what is our conclusion? It is this: there is no way we can get back into the Garden of Eden, and there is no *perfect* happiness to be found on this sin-stained planet either. Our only hope is the promise of heaven. That hope is meant to give our lives stability and substance. As Mark Buchanan says in his book *Things Unseen*, 'It is the Unseen Things that render the things we do see – both the beauty and the ugliness, the grandeur and the barrenness – never enough and yet never too much.'

FURTHER STUDY

Heb. 12:1-3;
Rev. 21:1-7,
22:1-7

1. Where should we fix our attention?

2. What are the key features of heaven?

Christian history shows that those who contributed the most in this present world were those who thought the most about the next. For instance, it was the apostles who set in motion the conversion of the Roman Empire, and it was the British evangelicals who abolished the slave trade. They left their mark on the world precisely because their minds were occupied with heaven. C.S. Lewis observed, 'It is since Christians have largely ceased to think of the other world that they have become so ineffective in this.'* Only those whose hearts and minds are filled with thoughts of heaven can relate to earth in a way that does not indulge either false Utopian dreams or despotic solutions.

To be of real earthly good requires us to be free from such fears as the fear of death, fear of the loss of property, or status, or comfort, or even our reputations. We should be like Stephen who, having willingly served meals to widows and confronted the stubborn and misunderstanding religious elements of his day, was able to look up to heaven at the moment of his death and see the glory of God.

Gracious, loving Father, as I turn from this theme to focus on other issues in the days ahead help me keep always before me the fact that heavenly mindedness will not detract from my effectiveness in this world but contribute to it. Amen.

* C.S. Lewis, *Mere Christianity*, © C.S. Lewis Pte. Ltd. (1942, 1943, 1944, 1952). Used by permission.

Heaven bent

FOR READING & MEDITATION - COLOSSIANS 3:1-17

'... set your hearts on things above, where Christ is seated at the right hand of God.' (v1)

In these closing days of this issue I have been trying to make clear that we need to embrace the fact that we are heaven bent. Our hearts have 'an inner tilt upward', as someone has put it. Those who belong to Jesus have a sure destination, and are given grace bigger than themselves to carry them towards that destination. There was a time when we were hell bent. Our personalities were bent all out of shape and we were certain of missing heaven. Now, because of Jesus, we have been redeemed and filled with a desire to see Him and be with Him in a perfect paradise.

The apostle Paul in today's text bids us set our hearts on things above. That suggests a determined, attentive gaze. Heaven is not something we should think about now and again; it is meant to be a *fixation*. The very thought of heaven should stir powerful feelings within us that enable us to leap over all obstacles.

Many years ago, when I was a pastor, I asked a group of Christians why they thought we do not make as much of heaven nowadays as Christians did in past generations. Many different replies were given but the consensus was this: we do not make as much of heaven as we should because we are afraid of being accused of avoiding our duties in this world – that it is possible to be so heavenly minded that we are no earthly good. That, of course, is true. However, some of the greatest contributors to society – John Wesley, for example, who had a keen social conscience – have been men and women who lived out their lives in the anticipation of eternity. When we recover the hope of the world without end and focus on it then we will discover that being heavenly minded makes us of much greater earthly good.

FURTHER STUDY

2 Cor. 12:1-6;
Titus 2:6-15

1. What did Paul boast about?

2. What should Christians be taught?

Father, how can I thank You enough that although once I was hell bent You have turned me around and now I am heaven bent? And grant that I shall become so heavenly minded that I will be of much greater earthly good. In Jesus' name. Amen.

Earth-oriented Christians

FOR READING & MEDITATION - COLOSSIANS 1:24-29
'... Christ in you, the hope of glory.' (v27)

The writer A.J. Conyers said, 'We live in a world no longer under heaven.' How often do you hear a sermon on the subject of heaven? Do you think much about it? Contemporary Christians are, it seems, much too earth-oriented and, as we said yesterday, have lost sight in their imagination of the world to come.

Listen to what John Eldridge says in his book *The Sacred Romance*: 'If for all practical purposes we believe that this life is our best shot at happiness, if this is as good as it gets, we will live as desperate, demanding and eventually despairing men and women. We will place on this world a burden that it was never intended to bear. We will try to find a way to get back into the Garden and when that fails, as it always does, our hearts fail as well.' It may sound as if he is talking to non-Christians but he is talking to believers whose only concern is to make something of life now – hence the desperation.

FURTHER STUDY

Luke 12:16-21;
1 Tim. 6:6-19

1. Why should we not be earth orientated?

2. What should we accumulate?

Am I saying Christians should stop pursuing a career or attempting to get a better home for themselves and their family? Of course not. If that is what you hear me saying then I have not made myself clear. There is nothing wrong with pursuing a career or buying a good home as long as we do not let those things fill our whole vision and lose sight of the fact that in this world we are exiles because our real home is in heaven. If I understand the Scriptures correctly, God wants us to live our lives in the anticipation of eternity, to lift our eyes beyond the immediate and have a clear vision of the kingdom that lies ahead. The sooner we focus on the things of eternity the better, otherwise we will turn out to be desperate and demanding people.

O God, I confess it is easier to keep my eyes on what is happening in this world than on the kingdom that lies ahead. Help me embrace eternal things, and give me a clearer understanding of their importance. In Jesus' name. Amen.

FOR READING & MEDITATION – COLOSSIANS 1:1-14

'... the faith and love that spring from the hope that is stored up for you in heaven ...' (v5)

We ended yesterday with the statement that even Christians are never *perfectly* satisfied in this world; we are always conscious when we tune in to what is going on inside us that there's more. We are, as we said, satisfied with an unsatisfied satisfaction.

Does that mean the words of Jesus 'I have come that they may have life, and have it to the full' recorded in John 10:10 is not true? No. Christians do have abundant life injected into their souls when they receive Him, but however wonderful and exhilarating it is, one senses that it does not produce *perfect* happiness. Our hearts still long for something even better. This is not to detract from the joy that Christ gives, but simply to say that in a fallen world, and in our fallen condition, we will never experience perfection in anything – the single exception being perfect in love (see Matt. 5:43–48).

Dr Martyn Lloyd-Jones once said, 'If I am looking for something in this life to make me *perfectly* happy and fulfilled then I am a carnal Christian.' Our hope for *perfect* happiness is never to be set on the things of time but on the things of eternity. Be honest now – where are your hopes for happiness set? Here or in the eternal future? Maturity, says a friend and colleague of mine, is knowing the difference between what we can get now and what we wait for. Paul tells us in Romans 8:23 that we have the first fruits (down payment) now, but the real harvest is yet to come. Our hearts cannot live without hope, and there is no greater hope, as today's text reminds us, than the prospect of one day being with our Father in heaven. We must never lose sight of the life that is to come.

FURTHER STUDY

1 Cor. 3:1-9;
1 John 2:15-17

1. What are the marks of a carnal or worldly Christian?

2. What shows we are focused on the life to come?

My Father and my God, quicken my imagination so that I will be able to focus more often on the hope that lies before me of being with Jesus for all eternity. In His peerless name I pray. Amen.

The joy of unfulfilment

FOR READING & MEDITATION - PHILIPPIANS 3:12-21

'But our citizenship is in heaven. And we eagerly await a Saviour from there, the Lord Jesus Christ ...' (v20)

Over the few remaining days of this issue we will consider this: why is it that most people at one time or another do not feel *at home* in this world? Charles Dickens, in a letter to a friend, expressed these thoughts: 'Why is it that a sense comes always crushing in on me now, when I fall into low spirits, as of one happiness I have missed in life, and one friend and companion I have never made?' Julian Huxley wrote, 'Sooner or later one asks even of Beethoven, even of Shakespeare: Is that all?' The human predicament is this: we can't sneak back into the Garden of Eden and no matter how happy our condition in this sin-cursed world there are feelings within us that say, 'I am made for something better than this.'

FURTHER STUDY

Psa. 27:1-14;
Heb. 11:8-16

1. What one thing did the psalmist seek?

2. Why was Abraham blessed but unfulfilled?

C.S. Lewis described this awareness so well when he wrote, 'You have never *had* it. All the things that have ever deeply possessed your soul have been hints of it – tantalising glimpses, promised but never quite fulfilled, echoes that died away just as they caught your ear. But if it should really become manifest – if ever there came an echo that did not die away but swelled into sound itself – you would know it. Beyond all possibility of doubt you would say: Here at last is the thing I was made for.'*

The joy of which Lewis speaks is not the joy of fulfilment or satisfaction but rather the joy of unfulfilment – the glimpse of something far off. One writer describes it as 'news from a country we have never visited'. This might sound strange, but even Christians are never perfectly satisfied in this world. We are satisfied with an unsatisfied satisfaction. We are in this world as exiles and all our senses cry out, 'This is not your home.' And strangely, we are glad.

O Father, forgive me for not always keeping in mind the truth that this world is not my home and that I'm just passing through. The things of time often blot out the things of eternity. Help me to have the right perspective on this issue. Amen.

* C.S. Lewis, *The Problem of Pain*, © C.S. Lewis Pte. Ltd. (1940). Used by permission.

Looking through 'seeing' eyes

FOR READING & MEDITATION - PSALM 73:1-28

'My flesh and my heart may fail, but God is the strength of my heart
and my portion for ever.' (v26)

We return to the issue we were considering before
Christmas Day and spend one last day thinking about
doubts which are deep, dark and potentially devastating.
Although we cannot stop what we are calling psychological
doubts arising in our minds, we can use them to ask the
hard questions that can cause us to take a firmer grip on
God. Doubts can be valuable if they motivate us to search
the Scriptures more thoroughly and come to God in more
fervent prayer.

The psalmist who wrote the psalm we have read today
appears to have been tested by the prosperity of
the wicked. He confesses that his feet had almost
slipped, but after confessing his doubts about the
justice of things he discovers a deep settled peace
in his soul. You may not be tested by the prosperity
of the wicked; with you perhaps it is something else
– a failure to find meaning in life or uncertainty
as to whether God is still in control of His world.
Whatever it is, keep in mind the powerful words of
Os Guinness to which I have already referred but
which I believe bear repeating: 'Doubt is a state
of mind between faith and unbelief so that it is neither of
them wholly and it is only each partly.' Throw yourself on
the side of faith. This is how God's people have overcome
their doubts throughout time – and when they have done so
they have then looked at things through 'seeing' eyes.

During the years that I have been a Christian I have
sometimes wondered to myself if anyone really rises to the
exhilaration and truth of the Christian faith who has not felt
first its incredibility, impossibility and sheer unbelievability.
When one realises it is all true then truly it is glory. Doubt
sets up assaults but faith brings about their defeat.

**FURTHER
STUDY**

2 Cor. 4:7-18;
1 Tim. 3:16;
Heb. 11:24-28

1. What did Paul
see and affirm?

2. What did
Moses see?

**O Father, give me eyes that see - really see. Through the eyes
of my soul help me recognise that though the world is fallen and
stained, ultimately justice will be done and all will be put right. In
Jesus' name. Amen.**

'Somebody with skin on'

FOR READING & MEDITATION - JOHN 1:1-18

'For the law was given through Moses; grace and truth came through Jesus Christ.' (v17)

We pause on this Christmas Day to drink in again the wonder of Jesus' coming to earth. Imagine what life in this fallen world would be like had He not come. Suppose, just suppose, that today's text simply read, 'The law was given through Moses,' and ended there. God's model and design for human life would thereafter have been contained in principles. Though principles are good they lack life. Picture a little child crying for his mother and being told, 'Don't cry little one, let me talk to you about the principle of motherhood.' The little child would still sob and say, 'I want my mummy.' You can't talk to a principle, you can only talk to a person.

FURTHER STUDY

Matt. 1:18-25; 1 John 1:1-9

1. What was significant about the baby's names?

2. What was John's testimony?

When we speak, as we have done over recent days, about grace flowing into our lives we need to remember that grace is not something God tips out of the sky. He *Himself* is grace. A little boy who was asked to connect the two words 'Jesus' and 'grace' replied, 'Jesus put a face on grace.' I wonder, did he realise the profundity of his reply? Grace is no longer something nebulous; it has form and reality. Grace comes to us through Jesus.

One little girl complained to her mother that she felt lonely at night. 'But you have your teddy bear,' said her mother. 'I know,' responded the little girl, 'but I want somebody with skin on.' When beset by life's problems we need something more than laws or principles; we want a person – somebody with skin on. Christmas focuses on the fact that when we link ourselves by faith to Jesus what we receive is not a principle or some vague inner trembling in our consciousness; what we receive is Jesus Himself. His coming was not limited to the first century. By His Spirit He is with us still. Grace!

Father, I am so glad that the grace revealed through the coming of Your Son that first Christmas is with us still. Thus the joy of Christmas Day should be with us every day. Thank you Father. Amen.

Honest doubts

FOR READING & MEDITATION – MATTHEW 11:1-15

'Are you the one who was to come, or should we expect
someone else?' (v3)

Yesterday we talked about defensive doubts. Today I
would like to examine with you the nature of honest
doubts. Honest doubts are those that are not a ploy of the
personality to get us off the hook as regards some moral
issue but arise because of a genuine intellectual concern.

Some Christians claim that when it comes to the truths
of Scripture or anything connected with God then a real
believer ought never to doubt. I would direct such Christians
to the passage we have read today. John the Baptist, you
remember, witnessed the descent of the Holy Spirit upon
Jesus Christ at His baptism and declared, 'Look,
the Lamb of God, who takes away the sin of the
world!' (John 1:29). Yet in these verses we see him
sending his disciples to Jesus with the question,
'Are you the one who was to come, or should we
expect someone else?' How did Jesus respond to
John's doubts? Did He say, 'Go back and tell John I
am disappointed in him for his doubts about me'?
No, He said, 'Go back and report to John what you
hear and see' (v4). He did not condemn him for his
doubts but responded to his question with love
and sensitivity.

**FURTHER
STUDY**

John 6:5-13;
James 1:5-8

1. How did
the disciples
express doubt?

2. What
happens if
we remain in
two minds?

Doubt, it must be remembered, is not the same
as unbelief. The writer, Os Guinness says, 'Doubt is a state
of mind between faith and unbelief so that it is neither of
them wholly and it is only each partly.' When we have an
honest doubt we are not betraying our faith or surrendering
to unbelief. We are simply saying we are in two minds –
and pondering which way to go. John used his doubt to ask
questions of Jesus. When you are in doubt I suggest that
you do the same. Ask questions of God and search for the
answers in Scripture. The Bible is a great remover of doubt.

**Father, how encouraging it is to learn that when I have an honest
doubt I am not surrendering to unbelief; it is rather that I am in
two minds. Help me to always make up my mind and come down
firmly on Your side in everything. Amen.**

Defensive doubts

FOR READING & MEDITATION – PSALM 51:1-19

'Surely you desire truth in the inner parts; you teach me wisdom in the inmost place.' (v6)

One of the things we should know about psychological doubt (doubt that does not necessarily come from the devil but arises from our marred image of God and a fallen world) is that there are two categories of this doubt – defensive doubt and honest doubt. Sometimes the doubts that arise within us which we think are connected to our faith are unconscious attempts to hide some moral weakness or failure. Let me illustrate.

As a young Christian I heard a challenging sermon that convicted me of the fact that there was a moral failure in my life. At that moment I came up against 'Brunner's Law' (a law attributed to a German Christian by that name) which states: the more a decision will affect your way of life the more your old nature will enter into the debate. My carnal nature supplied me with doubts which made me question whether the preacher had interpreted the passage of Scripture properly. I used these doubts to get myself off the hook. Rather than face the issue I preferred the safety of doubt. When I talked to my pastor he asked, 'If you really believed what you heard would you have to change anything in your life?' Immediately I saw what I was doing. I was using doubt as a defence. I preferred to convince myself that what I had heard was not a proper biblical exposition because to believe it meant I had to change.

FURTHER STUDY

Exod. 3:1-14;
Exod. 4:10-17

1. How did Moses express defensive doubt?

2. What was God's response?

Whenever you are assailed by doubts about the truth of Scripture ask yourself whether it is a ploy of your personality designed to get you off the hook as regards some personal challenge or whether it is an honest and genuine concern. This simple act of self-examination can sometimes resolve major issues.

Father, I accept that there is resistance within me that engenders self-deception and self-protection. Teach me by Your Spirit how to outwit and outmanoeuvre them. In Christ's name I pray. Amen.

FOR READING & MEDITATION – JOHN 20:24-31

'Then he said to Thomas, "Put your finger here ...
Stop doubting and believe."' (v27)

Without doubt (pardon the pun) the classic example of doubt in the Bible is the doubt displayed by the disciple Thomas. In fact, he is often referred to as *doubting* Thomas' – a rather unfair label if ever there was one. It's sad how we often pick on something negative in a person's life and make him or her carry that label for a lifetime, or, in the case of Thomas, two millennia. Thomas entered for a little while into the darkness of spiritual doubt but he emerged from that experience with a firmer faith than before.

There is some evidence that Thomas went to India to establish a Christian community, and that the 'St. Thomas Christians' are the spiritual descendants of those first converts. They are some of the finest and most dedicated Christians I have met. Thomas had his doubts allayed in one glorious act of illumination when he brought them to Jesus. Doubt assaulted him but was defeated. He became a believer and an achiever – and then he went places.

Some time ago l talked to a university student who said, 'Things are happening at such speed in the world. Old ideas are being demolished and replaced by new ones. I wake up every morning doubting that the Bible is true, and I am afraid that one day I will find science has completely disproved the Scriptures.' I assured him that his doubts were completely groundless for science – *true* science, that is – will never disprove Scripture, just confirm it. The God who created the universe and set in operation the laws of science is the God who inspired the writing of the Bible. This student seemed relieved by what I had to say, and I hope it relieves any doubts you may have on this subject too.

FURTHER STUDY

Mark 9:14-27;
Heb. 11:1-6

1. What was the doubting father's prayer?

2. What is the nature of faith?

O Father, whatever doubts may arise within me, help to bring them to the judgment bar of Holy Scripture. Teach me how to doubt my doubts and believe my beliefs. In Jesus' name. Amen.

Psychological doubts

FOR READING & MEDITATION – JUDE 17-23
'Be merciful to those who doubt ...' (v22)

We focus now on another matter which we have to deal with in a fallen world. I refer to having *doubts* which are deep, dark and awful. Earlier we saw how the devil used doubt as a strategy to bring about the downfall of Adam and Eve, but these doubts are not necessarily the 'fiery darts of the devil' but those that arise from our fallen condition. But not all our doubts are the result of the devil's deceit; many arise in our minds simply because our nature has been knocked off balance by Adam and Eve's sin so we don't think about life in the way God intended.

FURTHER STUDY

Judg. 6:1-24

1. What was Gideon's initial response to God's call?

2. How was God merciful to doubting Gideon?

These are what I am calling psychological doubts. But whatever the nature of your doubts, never let them remain. Deal with them right away by talking to an experienced minister or counsellor.

Some Christians seem never to have had a serious doubt in their lives. Over the years I have talked to countless believers who have told me that not once have they ever doubted God's Word, God's love, or any of His actions. But, on the other hand, I have also met hundreds of Christians who have told me of doubts so distressing that they have robbed them of sleep. Some Christians may have doubts about the divine inspiration of Scripture or the authenticity of the miracles. These are important matters which can be addressed. But some doubts are in a very different category. There are those who have doubts that cause them to question their own separateness and significance as a person or whether there is any meaning in this medley of experiences that we call 'life'. And remember: doubt is something more than a thought that is speculative and fleeting. Serious doubt grips you and holds you prisoner for weeks, months, and perhaps even years.

Father, help me to so fill my heart and mind daily with Your Word that it will never become a seed-bed for doubts which are deep, dark and awful. In Jesus' name I ask it. Amen.

Either way you win

FOR READING & MEDITATION - REVELATION 1:9-20

'I, John ... was on the island of Patmos because of the word of God and the testimony of Jesus.' (v9)

Two things need to happen when what we believe to be God-given plans lie crushed and broken. First, we need to learn to accept that God knows best and respond to the grace He gives by continuing to trust, worship and serve Him with all our heart. Second, we should stay alert to the fact that the shattered plans may be God's way of leading to an even bigger contribution to His kingdom.

When the apostle John found himself exiled to the island of Patmos because of his loyalty to the gospel it must have seemed that his ministry and all his plans had come to an end. The Moffatt translation of the Bible words our text for today thus: 'I John ... found myself on the island called Patmos, for adhering to God's word and the testimony of Jesus'. It continues, 'On the Lord's day I found myself rapt in the Spirit, and heard a loud voice ... calling, "Write your vision in a book"' (vv9–11). Isolated and prevented from preaching the gospel, John was used by God to write a book that has blessed and encouraged people throughout the centuries. The place of isolation became a place of revelation.

FURTHER STUDY

Dan. 3:16-30;
Acts 28:16-31

1. What was the attitude of the three Hebrews?

2. How did Paul win over false arrest and imprisonment?

Am I talking to someone today who is feeling dejected because of shattered hopes and plans? Don't allow yourself to sink. Instead receive the grace that is flowing towards you at this moment. It's the will of God that is important. Accept that fact. And since it is, you can rejoice in it and not simply resign yourself to it. Accept all things willingly. Be alert also to the possibility that this may be God's way of bringing you to the place where He will show you new and better plans. If no new plans are given then you will be given grace to handle the situation as it is. So either way you win.

Father, I am so thankful that in You I can always win. Surrendered to Your will, Your divine purposes are at work in me. Help me see that Your will is always best - no matter how things may appear. In Jesus' name. Amen.

Grace – like mighty Niagara

FOR READING & MEDITATION - 2 CORINTHIANS 6:1-13
'As God's fellow-workers we urge you not to receive
God's grace in vain.' (v1)

The mature Christian asks to be in God's will. He or she may desire success in every project undertaken for God, but they are not driven or controlled by the need for success. There is nothing wrong with desiring success, but there is everything wrong with demanding it.

Many of you may have heard of Henry Martyn, the famous missionary to India. Henry Martyn was born in Truro, Cornwall, and served in India as a chaplain with the East India Company, during which time he translated the New Testament into Hindustani. Later, in Iran, he translated the New Testament into Arabic and Farsi. His biographer tells how he once said, 'Let me labour for fifty years amidst scorn and never see one soul converted … the Lord Jesus who controls all events is my Friend, my Master, my God, my all.' From this it is obvious that he embarked upon his work with his eyes wide open to the possibility of not seeing the success he hoped and longed for. He would often quote the lines of a poem which was widely known in those days – a poem which contained these words:

FURTHER STUDY

2 Cor. 8:1-5;
Heb. 4:14-16

1. How did God's grace affect the Macedonian churches?

2. What is always available to us?

All as God wills
Who wisely heeds
To give or to withhold.

Maturity does not resist, pout or stamp its feet if God decides not to give outward signs of success. Rather, he or she accepts the fact that His grace flows as freely as the great and mighty Niagara, enabling His servant to trust and praise Him. And even though the things for which they have given their life lie broken and seem purposeless they avail themselves of God's grace and continue to serve Him.

Father, I am so thankful that nothing that happens here east of Eden can prevent Your grace reaching me. And it comes not merely as a trickle but as a flood. May that truth always be my comfort and my strength. In Jesus' name. Amen.

NEXT ISSUE

Songs for the Road

Start the New Year with an inspiring look at some special psalms. Written specifically to help prepare us for the year ahead, this issue of *Every Day with Jesus* leads us on a verse by verse study of Psalms 120 to 134.

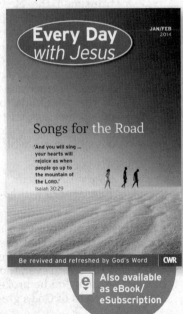

Known collectively as the Songs of Ascents, these fifteen psalms are thought by scholars to have been sung by Hebrew pilgrims on their way up to Jerusalem to celebrate the annual feasts. Combining uplifting praise and worship with practical insights, they provide a striking example of what it means to walk the road of faith.

Allow these psalms to fill you afresh with faith and praise as you move confidently into 2014.

Please note that from 2014 prices will increase to £2.99 per single issue. Subscription prices will remain unchanged.

Every Day with Jesus
JAN/FEB 2014

Songs for the Road

'And you will sing ... your hearts will rejoice as when people go up to the mountain of the LORD.'
Isaiah 30:29

Be revived and refreshed by God's Word   CWR

Also available as eBook/ eSubscription

OBTAIN YOUR COPY FROM
CWR, a Christian bookshop or National Distributor.
If you would like to take out a subscription, see the order form at the back of these notes.

Choose CWR for
Conferencing

CWR's two conference centres are ideal venues for church weekends and away days, leadership meetings, training events, weddings and other functions. Both are set in spacious grounds in peaceful countryside.

'the beautiful surroundings ... create an ideal atmosphere for a refreshing and inspiring time away.'

WAVERLEY ABBEY HOUSE
- Up to 100 delegates, 42 residentially
- 8 meeting/conference rooms
- Dining room, lounge and coffee bar with pool table
- Views across tranquil lake to woodland and ruins of ancient Waverley Abbey

Waverley Abbey House, Waverley Lane, Farnham, Surrey, GU9 8EP, UK
Call our Bookings Team on 01252 784733
or email waverley@cwr.org.uk

PILGRIM HALL
- Up to 125 delegates, 110 residentially
- 5 meeting rooms, lounges, and conservatory
- A wide range of indoor and outdoor activities
- Heated outdoor swimming pool (Summer months)

Pilgrim Hall, Easons Green, Uckfield, East Sussex TN22 5RE, UK
Call our Bookings Team on 01825 840295
or email bookings@pilgrimhall.com

www.cwr.org.uk/conferencing

The feel of eternal validity

FOR READING & MEDITATION - ROMANS 5:12-21

'... sin entered the world through one man, and death through sin, and in this way death came to all men ...' (v12)

Perhaps one of the hardest and most confusing things we have to face east of Eden is the fact of death – our own death or the death of a loved one. The curse that fell upon the earth means that everyone dies, as our text for today tells us. The only exceptions in Scripture were Enoch and Elijah. Of all the fears that invade the human heart probably the greatest is the fear of death.

One writer says, 'The fear of death is as *old* as human life, as *long* as human life and as *widespread* as human life.' Take the first statement: it is as *old* as human life. After God created Adam, one of the first things He said to him was this: 'You must not eat from the tree of the knowledge of good and evil, for when you eat of it you will surely die' (Gen. 2:17). Then consider the next statement: it is as *long* as human life. A person can be in their seventies or eighties and, if he or she is healthy and happy, still regard death as an unwelcome visitor. And we need no convincing that it is as *widespread* as human life for we know that it affects everyone – the rich and poor alike. George Bernard Shaw said, 'The statistics concerning death are very impressive – one out of every one dies!'

FURTHER STUDY

Psa. 103:1-22; Isa. 40:6-8

1. What did the psalmist acknowledge about God and himself?

2. What lasts for ever?

As I write this issue there is a war in the Middle East and war brings the fear of death once again to the forefront. Reactions to the subject of death are quite interesting. Some are unwilling to dwell on it at all and thrust it from their thoughts – it is plain they are in bondage and slavery to the fear of death. But though they can evade the thought they cannot evade the fact. Christians need have no fear of death since they have a life within them that survives death. Life before death guarantees life after death.

Father, I am so grateful that because of You I need have no fear of death. The life I live in You has the feel of eternal validity upon it. I am alive in Someone who will never die. Hallelujah!

'Sin's incinerator'

FOR READING & MEDITATION – 1 CORINTHIANS 15:50-58

'The sting of death is sin, and the power of sin is the law.' (v56)

Yesterday we talked about the fear of death being as *old*, as *long* and as *widespread* as human life. When we come to analyse fear of death certain facts emerge. Three elements, in the main, compose this fear. The first is the fear of the physical process of dying. This is a very real dread for people. Yet for many in today's world there is the consolation of knowing good pain control can dull the edge of the most excruciating pain. The second element of this fear is the fear of extinction – the dreadful thought that death is the end and that everything, including our loves and hopes, ends in a hole in the earth or in the flames of a crematorium.

The third element in the fear of death is the fear of judgment. This fear is not as strong as it once was since fewer people attend church, and also because statistics show that today fewer sermons are preached on the fact of judgment to come than at any other time in the past few hundred years. Yet a fear of judgment is there in every conscience. It finds support in the iron law of cause and effect and runs through all regulated life. Non-Christians in their more honest moments sense that God is a God of justice and often, as they near death, their conscience begins to awaken them to this possibility and they cry out for assurance.

But really only Jesus can give this assurance. To the honest He says, 'Your sins are forgiven you.' And it's all because of Calvary. 'The cross,' said someone, 'is sin's incinerator.' It is. No treatment is better for the fearful heart which shrinks from judgment than taking the names which describe the Saviour and piling them one upon the other: Redeemer! Deliverer! Friend!

FURTHER STUDY

Matt. 25:31-46; Luke 12:4-7

1. What separation happens after death?

2. What should people really fear about death?

Father, to analyse the fear of death is one thing; to overcome it is another. I am more grateful than words can convey that I live in a resurrected Christ. Since He lives eternally so shall I. Amen.

'The ten horses of evil'

FOR READING & MEDITATION - ROMANS 8:31-39

'... neither height nor depth, nor anything else in all creation, will ... separate us from the love of God ...' (v39)

In the passage before us today Paul tells us of ten things that cannot separate us from the love of God which is in Jesus our Lord. When he calls the roll of these ten things he identifies all the things that might break us here east of Eden: death, life, angels, demons, the present, the future, powers, height, depth, any other creature. In reality, Paul is saying, nothing can break you if you don't break with God.

Someone once described these ten things as 'the ten horses of evil' which attempt to ride us down and trample us with their feet. But because Jesus is with us, instead of these 'ten horses of evil' riding us down, we are able to grasp their bridles, swing into their saddles and ride them, making them go our way and not their way.

Take the first on Paul's list – *death*. He puts the worst first for death, as we have been saying, tops the list of human fears. William Randolph Hearst (1863–1951), an American media tycoon, would never allow anyone to speak of death in his presence. Just before she retired from his employment, his housekeeper – who was a Christian – confronted him and said, 'Mr Hearst, I know you don't like talking about death, but I want you to know that I am looking forward to it.' Hearst replied, 'How can you look forward to death? You don't know what lies on the other side.' 'I don't know *what* lies on the other side,' she responded, 'but I know *who* is there – my Lord and Saviour, Jesus Christ.' Then she added, 'And that's good enough for me.' In the risen and living Christ she knew she had immortality, for the pulse of immortality was already beating in her.

FURTHER STUDY

Psa. 23:1-6;
Rom. 14:7-9

1. What was the psalmist's conviction?

2. How did Paul view life and death?

O deathless Jesus, alive for evermore, why should I be afraid of death? I am in You and death is merely a transition - it is like stepping onto the veranda that opens to the House of Many Rooms. I am so grateful. Amen.

God's will – always best

FOR READING & MEDITATION – ROMANS 12:1-8

'... I urge you ... in view of God's mercy, to offer your bodies as living sacrifices, holy and pleasing to God ...' (v1)

Today I would like to pose a question that is often debated in Bible colleges and among Christian workers: Is it a sign of spiritual immaturity in us if we *must* see success? Everyone longs for success when embarking upon a spiritual calling, especially when they are convinced their desire is of God. But can we be more committed to the idea of success than to doing the will of God?

There have been a good number of spiritual successes in my life (and some disappointments also). But I wonder how I would have handled an apparent failure – especially the failure of what I considered to be an important spiritual project. Take *Every Day with Jesus*, for example. In 1965 God called me to write a daily devotional by quickening a verse from the book of Revelation to my heart: 'Write ... what you have seen' (Rev 1:19). In 2015, God willing, CWR will be celebrating 50 years of life-changing ministry. What if, say, 20 years ago the whole project had failed and I was therefore unable to continue writing it? And what if during my prayer time God had said to me, 'That's the end of your writing career. My purpose for you now is to tend this plot for Me where your name will not be known and you will reach just a few dozen people'? How would I have reacted?

FURTHER STUDY

Hab. 3:11-19;
Matt. 14:1-12

1. How can we explain the prophet rejoicing in calamity?

2. How can we explain the murder of John?

The answer is that I just don't know. Hopefully I would have risen to the challenge and been concerned only about being in God's will. However, from talking to others who have been in the situation of finding their life plans crushed I know that would not have been easy. All I can say with certainty is that there is grace available to meet every situation. Our challenge is to lay hold of it.

Father, it's so easy to say that Your will is always best, but not so easy to live through the experience of having our plans for success thwarted. O deepen my conviction that You always give the best to those who leave the choice to You. Amen.

Triumphing in trust

FOR READING & MEDITATION – GENESIS 50:15-21

'You intended to harm me, but God intended it for good to accomplish what is now being done ...' (v20)

It's not easy, as we said yesterday, living in a world where even what one considers to be a God-guided mission can end in seeming failure. Some people, like Joseph, live to see the dark mysteries of their lives cleared up while still on earth. Sold by his brothers into slavery, slandered by a lascivious woman, thrown unjustly into prison, he might well have felt utterly forsaken by God. Later, though, his belief in God's care over him was vindicated in the sight of everyone and he was able to say to his brothers, 'What you meant for harm God meant for good' (paraphrased). But what about those men and women who pass from this world without being vindicated, who die apparent failures?

Some Christians are able to maintain an unshaken trust in God even when what they considered to be divinely given plans lie broken all around them. Recently I have been reading a biography of a little known missionary by the name of Allen Gardiner who travelled to Tierra del Fuego in South America with six companions to found a mission. Due to lack of food, one after the other died. Yet Gardiner, in his diary, wrote just days before he passed away, 'Great and marvellous are the loving-kindnesses of my gracious God to me. He has preserved me hitherto and for four days, although without bodily food, without any feeling of hunger and thirst.' Not even the complete failure of what he regarded as a God-given plan could rob him of trust. He asked only to be in God's will, and if God's will led to no outward signs of success he did not complain. Instead he demonstrated the attitude of Job who said, 'Though he slay me, yet will I hope in him' (Job 13:15).

FURTHER STUDY

Job 2:7-10;
Heb. 11:29-40

1. What point did Job make to his wife?

2. How might faith reveal itself?

O Father, how I long for a faith like this that triumphs in the face of everything. I cannot raise such faith by my own efforts. It must come from You. Give me that kind of faith I pray. In Jesus' name. Amen.

When plans go wrong

FOR READING & MEDITATION - PSALM 88:1-18

'You have taken my companions and loved ones from me;
the darkness is my closest friend.' (v18)

Another bitter consequence of living in a world that is fallen is *the pain of shattered hopes and broken plans*. Christian history is full of stories of God's servants following what they believed was His guidance only to find events did not work out as planned.

On a visit to East Africa I was reminded of the story of James Hannington who landed in Zanzibar in 1882. Less than a year later he was forced by illness to return to England. After he had recovered he was consecrated first bishop of Eastern Equatorial Africa in 1884. But just nine months after arriving in Mombasa he was speared to death while attempting to enter Uganda. Many were puzzled by this and wondered why God could allow such an enterprise to fail. It's one of those mysteries that we will only understand in eternity.

FURTHER STUDY

Psa. 80:1-19;
Psa. 137:1-7

1. What was the psalmist's lament?

2. How had the people's hopes been crushed?

Some failures, of course, can be turned to advantage, as we shall see, but how are we to explain those situations where people gave their lives for what they believed was a God-guided cause only to find their plans were broken and apparently purposeless? One missionary known to me took his family to what was then the Belgian Congo but had to return within a year because he caught a disease that paralysed him for life. A few years ago I saw him at a conference sitting in a wheel chair and asked him how he was. He said, 'This mystery of how I went to the mission field and all my plans were turned upside down may never get cleared up while still on earth. I spend much of my time where the psalmist was when he wrote Psalm 88: "darkness is my closest friend".' It's not easy living in a world where life's plans can go so wrong.

Father, I don't have to face this kind of problem here east of Eden, but if I do then be the light in my darkness I pray. And I ask that You will be with those who may be facing this problem right now. In Jesus' name. Amen.

Fully dressed

FOR READING & MEDITATION - EPHESIANS 6:10-20

'... put on the full armour of God, so that when the day of evil comes, you may be able to stand your ground ...' (v13)

We have been seeing that one of the consequences of living in a fallen world is that we face accusations from the devil himself. God, however, has given us a defence against Satan and his lies and deceit. As we see from today's reading He has provided us with equipment.

First, we can wear the belt of truth which is acquired by meditating on His Word. Then He has given us a breastplate of righteousness – the conviction that we are saved not by our own righteousness but by His. Third, we have our feet shod with the readiness that comes from the gospel of peace – a determination to stand firm on the teaching of the gospel. Fourth, we are able to raise the shield of faith by quickly resisting the devil's lies and replacing them with God's truth. Fifth, we put on the helmet of salvation by living in the assurance that we are saved not only from the penalty of sin but also from its power and, one day in the future, from its very presence. All these things are our defence. So to go on the offensive we also need the sword of the Spirit, which is the Word of God. With this we are able to rebut the lies and temptations of the devil in the same way that Jesus did in the midst of His temptation in the wilderness.

FURTHER STUDY

James 4:1-7;
1 Pet. 5:1-11;
1 John 2:12-14

1. What precedes resisting the devil?

2. How can we overcome the evil one?

It is important to note this too: it is not enough to put on this spiritual armour; we are instructed to 'pray in the Spirit on all occasions'. Praying in the Spirit means praying in the power of the Spirit – not relying on our ability to pray or put words together but acknowledging our complete dependence on the Spirit to guide and empower our praying. Dressed like this, no one need be afraid of the devil. He will be afraid of you.

Gracious Father, help me understand more deeply what is involved in putting on the armour You have provided for me against Satan and his forces. And may I never attempt to deal with him unless I am fully dressed. In Jesus' name. Amen.

Satan's chief weapon

FOR READING & MEDITATION - JOHN 8:42-47

'When he lies, he speaks his native language, for he is a liar and the father of lies.' (v44)

Today we ask ourselves: How does the devil go about the task of attacking God's people? His major weapon is always that of deceit. This is how he achieved success in bringing about the downfall of Adam and Eve – and it is his chief weapon still. There are many ways by which we can be deceived but I would like to look with you today a little more closely at the thrust of the original temptation levelled at Adam and Eve as I think the strategy used then, which proved so successful, is one that he continues using to this very day.

FURTHER STUDY

Gen. 3:1-14;
Luke 4:1-13

1. What three things attracted Eve to eat the fruit?

2. How might Satan use God's own words to trick us?

Satan did not attempt to get Adam and Eve to become atheists because he knew that was an impossibility. So he focused instead on getting them to doubt God's goodness. The devil began by saying, 'Did God really say, "You must not eat from any tree in the garden?"' (Gen. 3:1). That question was formed in such a way that it introduced the first human pair to something they had not come up against before – an attack on the character of God. Eve then explained the situation, and this gave the devil further opportunity to sow doubt on God's goodness. 'You will not surely die,' he said (Gen. 3:4). The implication behind these words was the suggestion that if God really loved them He would not have limited them in that way.

Have you, I wonder experienced something similar in your own life? Have you been tempted to doubt God by someone suggesting that if God really loved you He would not have let that thing happen to you – your marriage difficulties, your child taking drugs, your financial problems, your serious sickness? Stay alert to Satan's use of this, his chief weapon.

Gracious and loving Father, help me resist all attacks on Your character and to accept that all Your purposes for me are good – even when, to human reasoning, they seem to be otherwise. In Jesus' name. Amen.

Everyone a soldier

FOR READING & MEDITATION - 1 TIMOTHY 6:11-21
'Fight the good fight of the faith.' (v12)

All who have committed their lives to Jesus Christ know, or should know, that there are in existence two orders and two kingdoms, the forces of which are locked together in fierce combat. One is the kingdom of God and the other is the kingdom of the devil. And Christians, whether they like it or not, are thrust right into the front line.

Many Christians (and, of course, non-Christians also) are pacifists when it comes to the matter of earthly warfare. But no one can be a pacifist when it comes to the matter of spiritual warfare. Once we enlist in the army of God then we engage in offensive and defensive spiritual warfare. At times in the Christian life we will find ourselves in a conflict that demands hand-to-hand combat with the forces of darkness, and unless we are prepared for these situations we can easily be overthrown. The Bible makes clear that the devil and his minions are bitter enemies of God, but because they are powerless against Him they turn their attention on those who are His followers – you and me.

FURTHER STUDY

2 Cor. 10:1-5;
Eph. 2:1-7;
Col. 1:10-14

1. What are the weapons of our warfare?

2. What journey have we already made?

The apostle Paul said, 'For our struggle is not against flesh and blood, but against the rulers, against the authorities, against the powers of this dark world and against the spiritual forces of evil in the heavenly realms' (Eph. 6:12). Have you ever noticed how many times the word 'against' appears in that passage? It occurs five times in all, indicating that when a person comes over on to the side of Jesus Christ he or she is immediately identified as being *for* God and *against* the devil. There can be no compromise on this issue, no peaceful co-existence pact, no give and take. Again I say it: to be *for* God is to be *against* the devil.

Father, I see that there is no safety zone in a universe in which every square inch is claimed by You and counter-claimed by the devil. Help me to fight against the devil and all his forces. In Jesus' name. Amen.

Know your enemy

FOR READING & MEDITATION - MATTHEW 4:1-11

'Then the devil left him, and angels came and attended him.' (v11)

Yesterday we said that some Christians do not believe in a personal devil; they see evil as more of an influence than coming from an evil being. If proof is needed of a personal devil then consider the passage we have read today. Jesus is seen here in direct confrontation with the devil, even engaging in conversation with him.

Liberal theologians (those whom I think of as having put their thoughts above God's thoughts) say that what Christ was doing here was engaging with the dark thoughts within Him, so any 'devil' present was subjective rather than objective. If Jesus did have 'dark thoughts' within His nature then the whole scheme of redemption crumbles, for a Saviour who is not perfect could never atone for our sins. Bishop Handley Moule, a great Bible expositor and a strong evangelical, said, 'A Saviour who is not perfect and who is not God is like a bridge broken at the farther end.' Once we try to get around Scripture and refuse to accept the plain truth of the Word of God then we create endless difficulties for ourselves. Let it be understood at once that for a Christian, life east of Eden means that we are involved in a conflict not only against sin but also against Satan.

FURTHER STUDY

Zech. 3:1-2;
2 Cor. 2:5-11

1. What was Satan doing to the high priest?

2. Of what was Paul aware?

The first principle of warfare, such as that currently being waged in the Middle East, is to know your enemy. Well, in spiritual terms, we too are at war. Our enemy is Satan, and the more we know about his wiles the more effective we will be in combating him. The evil influence that is in the world comes directly from an evil being. Add the letter 'D' to evil and you find the truth.

Father, I ask again that I may not be misled by Satan's accusations. I know he would like to get me not to believe in him. Show me the truth. In Jesus' name I ask this. Amen.

Is there a personal devil?

FOR READING & MEDITATION - JOHN 10:1-10

'The thief comes only to steal and kill and destroy ...' (v10)

Yet another issue that we have to cope with as a consequence of living in a fallen world is that of *accusation of the devil* himself. Satan's success in procuring the fall of Adam and Eve, and the chaos that occurred as a result of their sin, no doubt emboldened him in his quest to destroy the whole human race. Jesus, in the passage before us today, exposes the devil's 'mission statement': he comes 'to steal and kill and destroy'.

Surprisingly to me, there are some Christians who don't believe in a personal devil. A modern-day theologian writes, 'Let us put to sleep this idea of a personal devil who walks about with a pitchfork seeking to tumble people into hell. Evil is not a personality, but an influence – the darkness where the light ought to be.' Whilst I agree that the picture of a personal devil with horns and a tail walking about with a pitchfork is not to be found anywhere in Scripture, the concept of a personal devil is found everywhere in Scripture. The very names given to him denote personality: Satan, Deceiver, Liar, Murderer, Accuser, Tempter, Ruler of the kingdom of the air, and so on. An old rhyme says this:

**FURTHER
STUDY**

1 Chron. 21:1-8;
Job 1:6-22

1. What caused
David to sin?

2. What caused
Job's loss
and pain?

> *Men don't believe in the devil now as their fathers used
> to do;*
> *They reject one creed because it's old for another
> because it's new;*
> *They say the devil has never lived, or the devil
> has been and gone,*
> *But simple people would like to know – who carries
> his business on?*

Whether or not you believe in the devil he believes in you.

Father, help me see that it is to the devil's advantage to persuade me not to believe in him; then he can do his evil work unresisted. Help me get my perspective clear on this important issue. In Jesus' name. Amen.

A word of caution

FOR READING & MEDITATION - HEBREWS 13:1-6

'... God has said, "Never will I leave you; never will I forsake you."'
(v5)

Before we leave this subject of the hiddenness of God it is important to understand that the sense of God's absence may sometimes be due to some reason other than poor choices or that God has withdrawn His hand so that we might stand on our own two feet. It could be due to a physical problem.

One of the great challenges I have found when counselling is to discern the difference between what may be a physical problem that is affecting the spirit and what may be an issue arising from the spirit. For example, a woman once told me that she felt abandoned by God, but as we talked about her general health it became clear that she was in need of a physical checkup. I suggested this to her and her doctor diagnosed hypoglycemia – low blood sugar. Once this was corrected she felt her usual self again. It was not a spiritual issue – the 'hiddenness of God' – that was causing the difference in her but a physical problem that was pressing on her spirit. Physical conditions can produce symptoms that give the appearance of being spiritual or emotional problems, and we would be wise to always consider this. The physical can affect the spiritual just as the spiritual can affect the physical.

FURTHER STUDY

1 Kings 19:1-10;
John 14:15-27

1. What was God's immediate remedy for Elijah's depression?

2. What did Jesus promise?

The final thing I would like to say about this matter of 'the hiddenness of God' is that though God may appear to be hidden, His love for you is unfailing and never ceases. Never forget that. He hasn't really left you; it only seems that way. Heed these words of an unknown poet:

> *Behind the dim unknown,*
> *Standeth God within the shadow,*
> *Keeping watch above His own.*

O Father, give me the trust that my Saviour had on the cross when, although conscious of Your absence, He was still able to commit His spirit into Your hands. In His precious name I pray. Amen.

Prepared for ministry

FOR READING & MEDITATION - PSALM 102:1-28

'Do not hide your face from me when I am in distress.' (v2)

New Christians are sometimes confused because immediately after their conversion God's presence is so new and fresh. A new Christian may feel aliveness in their spirit – but maybe after a time they become all too familiar with and less conscious of God's Spirit. Then they attempt to stand on their own two feet in order to carry out His will and purpose.

Referring once again to C.S. Lewis's *Screwtape Letters*, he has the senior devil describe the phenomenon of abandonment in this way: 'He leaves the creature to stand up on its own legs – to carry out from the will alone duties which have lost all relish.'* The 'hiddenness of God' may be painful for the soul, but something is being accomplished in the silence that is worth much more than the cost.

A Catholic theologian tells how in a dream he saw Jesus approach three nuns who were at prayer. The Lord bent down and spent a good deal of time telling the first nun that He loved her. He did something similar with the second nun, but spent a little less time with her. However, He seemed to ignore the third nun because He simply passed her by without even a word. The man remembered thinking in his dream that the third nun had in some way offended Jesus, but it was impressed upon him that she was the most favoured. And why? Because God had a particular work for her to do which would involve a deep and abiding trust, and the only way she would be prepared for that was to learn how to obey even though God appeared to be absent. In the silence she was growing into the kind of person God wanted her to be.

FURTHER STUDY

Psa. 42:1-11;
James 1:1-12

1. What was the psalmist's remedy for abandonment?

2. How should we respond to trials of faith?

Father, I see that though Your 'hiddenness' may be painful for the soul, the rewards are greater than the cost. Burn this truth deeply into my spirit so that it will remain with me the rest of my life. In Jesus' name. Amen.

* C.S. Lewis, *The Screwtape Letters*, © C.S. Lewis Pte. Ltd. (1942). Used by permission.

FOR READING & MEDITATION – JOB 13:20-27

'Why do you hide your face and consider me your enemy?' (v24)

Why do God's children go through the experience of feeling abandoned by Him? We wondered the other day whether perhaps it is to test if we trust God in the dark, if we walk by faith and not by sight. After pondering this matter for many years I have come to the conclusion that it is.

C.S. Lewis, in *The Screwtape Letters* (imaginary instructions by a senior devil to a junior devil), bears down on this point and has the senior devil say this to his apprentice: 'Now it may surprise you to learn that in His efforts to get permanent possession of a soul He [God] relies on the troughs even more than the peaks; some of His special favourites have gone through longer and deeper troughs than anyone else. The reason is this ... the obedience the Enemy demands of men is quite a different thing ... He really does want to fill the universe with a lot of loathsome replicas of Himself – creatures whose life on its miniature scale will be qualitatively like His own, not because He has absorbed them but because their wills freely conform to His.'*

FURTHER STUDY

2 Cor. 1:3-11; 2 Cor. 4:7-18

1. How did Paul endure unendurable suffering?

2. Why did he not lose heart?

There is nothing that riles the devil and his minions more than seeing a man or woman who feels that every trace of God has vanished continuing to obey the Lord despite feeling abandoned. It is through descending into such 'troughs' that a Christian grows into the kind of person God wants him or her to be. The story of Job, of course, provides the supreme example of this. The extreme 'troughs' through which Job went provided new opportunities for knowing God in a deeper way. As a result he grew into the man God intended him to be – someone who could walk by faith and not by sight.

O Father, help me remember if I ever find myself in such a 'trough' that it is not a sign of Your disappointment in me but of Your favour. No matter what happens I long to be the person You want me to be. In Jesus' name. Amen.

* C.S. Lewis, *The Screwtape Letters*, © C.S. Lewis Pte. Ltd. (1942). Used by permission.

Love Came to Bring us Home

a further journey

We know that 'Love came to bring us home'. We know that God is there to walk beside us through the maze of life. But we also know that we will face struggles and difficulties during that journey. *EDWJextra* is a free online resource for small group study which can further enhance your understanding of this topic.

EDWJextra offers:

A short video which sets the scene introduced by Mick Brooks, the Consulting Editor for *Every Day with Jesus*.

Printable material is provided by Ian Sewter, author of the Further Study sections on each day of your *Every Day with Jesus* notes. Ian helps readers to explore the theme using:

· icebreakers
· summaries of the readings
· discussion starters
· prayer points
· key scriptures on which to meditate.

Visit www.cwr.org.uk/edwjextra to download the November/December *EDWJExtra* and for details of bulk discounts for groups following *Every Day with Jesus*.

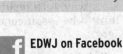

EDWJ on Facebook
Why not join in the conversation at
www.facebook.com/edwjpage

Christ's cry of dereliction

FOR READING & MEDITATION - MARK 15:33-41

'... Jesus cried out in a loud voice ... "My God, my God, why have you forsaken me?"' (v34)

The experience of feeling abandoned by God is more common than most people think. You have only to read the biographies of honest Christian leaders of the past to discover that many of them experienced this.

Take David Brainerd, for example, the great missionary who ministered in the eighteenth century to the North American Indians. One day he wrote these words in his *Journal*: 'I have no fellow Christian to whom I might unburden myself, or lay open my spiritual sorrows, with whom I might take sweet counsel in conversation about heavenly things and join in social prayer. My labour is hard and extremely difficult and I have little appearance of success to comfort me ... but what makes all my difficulties grievous to be borne *is that God hides His face from me*.' More than once he cried, 'I mourned after the presence of God and seemed like a creature banished from His sight.'

FURTHER STUDY

Psa. 22:1-21;
Isa. 54:6-8

1. How did the psalmist combine abandonment and faith?

2. How long may we feel abandoned and accepted by God?

We know from today's reading that Jesus felt abandoned by His Father as He hung upon the cross. We hear His cry of dereliction shiver to the sky. There is an ongoing debate among Bible students as to whether the Father actually abandoned His Son on the cross or whether the Son only *felt* abandoned. We can argue one way or the other but one thing is sure: the Saviour knows what it is like to *feel* abandoned by the Father. This can, however, provide encouragement for those who are undergoing this experience. Thousands of believers, both in the past and the present, have discovered that though for a time they felt abandoned, the moment came when they were conscious of Him being gloriously near again and could commend their spirit to Him.

O Father, something in me shrinks from ever having to experience a sense of divine abandonment, but if You call me to go this way then help me remember that my feelings are not the reality. In Jesus' name. Amen.

The hiddenness of God

FOR READING & MEDITATION – PSALM 10:1-18

'Why, O LORD, do you stand far off? Why do you hide yourself in times of trouble?' (v1)

We consider now another hard thing we have to bear in a fallen world – *dereliction*. By this I mean a sense of feeling abandoned by God which is sometimes called 'the dark night of the soul'. The feeling of being deserted by the One who has been trusted is the darkest and most difficult experience for a believer east of Eden.

It seems rather strange that the God who promises His children that He will never leave us or forsake us sometimes allows us to experience a sense of abandonment. Theologians sometimes speak of this as 'the hiddenness of God'. It is one thing to feel that God has withdrawn His presence because of some known and unconfessed choice, but it is quite another to feel that He has withdrawn Himself inexplicably. If we know God has withdrawn Himself because of our sin then it is a matter of confessing it, asking for and receiving divine forgiveness, certain that when we have done so we will experience the nearness of His presence once again. But if we do not know why He has withdrawn Himself then how can we ensure that we feel His presence once more? This is the dark dilemma in which God's people have sometimes found themselves.

FURTHER STUDY

Psa. 13:1-6;
Psa. 30:6-12

1. Describe the thoughts of the psalmist.

2. Contrast his feelings of security and abandonment.

Judging by what we have read today the psalmist seems to have gone through this experience. Yet by the time he ends the psalm he is affirming the fact that God does see trouble and grief and is a Father to the fatherless. There must be some deep divine purpose in an experience such as this. Is it perhaps to test whether or not we trust God in the dark, if we walk by faith and not by sight? If it is then the psalmist appears to have made that transition. Blessed are they who will not let go in the dark what they found in the light.

My Father and my God, if I am called to go this way then please help me to pass the test I pray. May I never let go in the darkness what I have discovered in the glow and realisation of Your divine presence. In Jesus' name. Amen.

Jesus! Jesus! Jesus!

FOR READING & MEDITATION - HEBREWS 4:14-16

'For we do not have a high priest who is unable to sympathise with our weaknesses ...' (v15)

It is one thing to face the prospect of one's own death, but it is another to face the death of a loved one. I know there will be many reading these lines who are in that situation right now. Bereavement is not too hard to bear when our dear ones are full of years and ready for heaven. As one writer says, 'The mellow fruit falls and we have grace to bear the pang. Heaven next.' But to lose a wife or a husband or a child whilst still comparatively young needs a double supply of grace. Someone has said that the death of parents is the death of the past, the death of a husband or wife is the death of the present, the death of a child is the death of the future.

FURTHER STUDY

2 Sam. 12:16-23;
Acts 4:10-12;
Phil. 2:5-11

1. What was David's response to his son's death?

2. What is special about the name of Jesus?

Am I speaking today to someone who is mourning the recent loss of a loved one? Let me speak as someone who has been there, having lost my wife to cancer, my father just three weeks later, and in recent years my only two sons. For a while it may seem as if you are walking in the darkness and you don't even know how to put words together to pray. When my two sons died, even though I form prayers for people to follow each day here in *Every Day with Jesus*, somehow I couldn't put together a prayer for myself. I found, however, that when I simply said 'Jesus' there was no need to worry about forming a prayer. I would utter the name 'Jesus' a hundred times during the day and also when I lay awake at night. Just that one word said over and over again – 'Jesus, Jesus, Jesus' – was more powerful than the most eloquently formed prayer. It never failed to bring God incredibly close. The old song 'His name is as ointment poured forth' is more than poetry; what it says is absolutely true. The One who wept at the grave of His friend Lazarus feels also for you.

Lord Jesus Christ, You who wept at the grave of Your friend Lazarus, I know You are there to comfort me in my times of grief and sadness. Your name truly 'is as ointment poured forth'. Blessed, blessed Jesus. Amen.

'His *Father's* house'

FOR READING & MEDITATION - HEBREWS 2:1-18

'... and free those who all their lives were held in slavery by their fear of death.' (v15)

Our text for today confirms what we have been saying, namely that many are held in slavery by the fear of death. Thus the question is of critical importance: How then can we be delivered from the slavery that the fear of death brings? The answer for us is to keep in mind that Jesus has promised to give us peace concerning everything – if we open ourselves to Him. Christians who carry in their hearts a fear of death are like those who have been left a large legacy but never come forward to claim it. He who conquered sin has conquered death.

One poet, speaking of death, described it as 'the undiscovered country from which no traveller has returned'. Well, Jesus has returned. To those Christians who still shrink before what they see as the grim 'angel of death' I would say this: think of death as having one mission – to lead us into our Father's immediate presence and give us an abiding place amongst those who knew Christ and have gone on before.

It is true that Jesus did not tell us much about heaven but what He did say was very significant. 'In my Father's house,' He informed us, 'are many rooms' (John 14:2). What did He call it? 'My *Father's* house.' Ought that not to be enough to settle or dismiss all our fears? Jesus is going to take us to His Father's house. And bear in mind that after His resurrection Jesus told Mary Magdalene, 'I am returning to my Father and *your* Father' (John 20:17). So allow this thought to grip you now: Jesus' Father is *your* Father. Let us therefore live here on earth with a sense of childlike anticipation, knowing that when our lives are complete we are going to dwell in our Father's house for evermore.

FURTHER STUDY

John 14:1-4;
2 Cor. 5:1-10;
Phil. 1:20-26

1. What is Jesus' ministry in heaven?

2. Where is our true home?

Lord Jesus, had You stalled at the last obstacle – death – then we would be stalled eternally. Now we need have no fear for You, who are true in every word, every deed, would not foist on us a lie. Thank You dear Father. Amen.